The Systems Thinking Approach™
to

THE ABCs
of
STRATEGIC
MANAGEMENT™
Planning • Leadership • Change

An

Executive Briefing

and

"Plan-to-Plan" Day

on

Strategic Management

in the 21st Century

by
Stephen G. Haines

President and Founder, the Centre for Strategic Management®

1420 Monitor Road • San Diego • California • 92110-1545 • (619) 275-6528 • Fax (619) 275-0324

Copyright © 2005
The ABCs of Strategic Management: Planning, Leadership, and Change
Systems Thinking Press®
3rd Edition, Revision 11
Second Printing
Library of Congress Control Number: 2004102043
ISBN: 0-9719159-7-0

Note on Trademarks

The following Trademarks (™) are licensed to Systems Thinking Press and the Centre for Strategic Management® and may not be used without explicit written permission. All Trademarks must carry this mark (™) and be specifically attributed to the Centre for Strategic Management® (www.csmintl.com):

- Achieving Leadership Excellence™
- Business Excellence Architecture™
- Creating the People Edge™
- Enterprise-Wide Change™
- Quadruple Bottom Line™
- Reinventing Strategic Planning™

- Rollercoaster of Change™
- Smart Start™
- Strategic IQ™
- The ABCs of Strategic Management™
- The Simplicity of Systems Thinking™
- The Systems Thinking Approach™

EBRSP-Cover.pmd

1420 Monitor Road • San Diego • California • 92110-1545 • (619) 275-6528 • Fax (619) 275-0324

> The future has always been difficult to handle, so . . .
> it is really a challenge that requires a broad input.
> Companies and industries die because
> executives did not think of what is yet to come.
>
> —*Adapted from P. Crosby*
>
> Plans are nothing.
> Planning is everything.
>
> —*Dwight D. Eisenhower*

The Centre's "Nothing to Lose" Guarantee
How to Get Started on Your Strategic Management Process
"Value-Added" One-Day Meeting

Dear Participant:

As a way to get started on your Customer Value, Strategic Planning or Enterprise-Wide Change Process, we usually recommend a one-day Executive Briefing and Plan-to-Plan session with the Centre for Strategic Management®. This one day is dedicated to educating participants on either (1) strategic planning, (2) creating customer value, or (3) any large scale change project you are planning to implement. It allows us to get on the same page with your situation. We will also mutually analyze, decide, and tailor what type of strategic planning or change management project, if any, should go beyond this one day event. Along with our 4-color Strategic Planning/ Strategic Change Systems Model, this booklet is the handouts and overheads we use in this 1-day session.

We are so confident of our ability to help you in this one day that we offer a **"Nothing to Lose" Guarantee** for this event with your top management team. If you do not get a "Value-Added" day from the time we spend together, pay us our expenses only and the day's fee is waived.

In addition, there is **No Further Obligation** beyond the one day . . . both parties have to agree that there is mutual benefit to proceed further.

As a prework to this Booklet and Plan-to-Plan Day, we highly recommend you first read our 4-page Executive Summary Article entitled, *The ABCs of Strategic Management*℠. Without the article and Model, this booklet will not be as useful and user friendly to you. If you need a copy of this article or Model, please call us at the Centre.

Happy Reading,

Stephen S. Haines

Stephen G. Haines, President
San Diego, California
(619) 275-6528 — **www.csmintl.com**

P.S. For more related Strategic Management products, please see our publishing division at www.SystemsThinkingPress.com

EBRSP-Cover.pmd

REINVENTING STRATEGIC PLANNING

TABLE OF CONTENTS

"The Key to Successful Strategic Management"

#1: Focus — Set Priorities — Focus

#2: The only alternative to perseverance is failure.

1420 Monitor Road • San Diego • California • 92110-1545 • (619) 275-6528 • Fax (619) 275-0324

EXECUTIVE BRIEFING ON THE ABCs OF STRATEGIC MANAGEMENT™

ONE DAY OFFSITE MEETING — INCLUDING PLAN-TO-PLAN SESSION

A.M. Main Purposes: Educating

1. To gain a common set of principles and knowledge about the three main premises for the successful reinventing of strategic planning concepts.

2. To identify the three goals of strategic planning; to recognize that planning is really one part of a three-part Strategic Management System (SMS); to learn what that really means, as the #2 required Core Competency of every organization in the world!

3. To understand how to design, build, and sustain (i.e., create) a *High Performance Organization for the 21st Century* through our Systems Thinking Approach™ that guides our "Business Excellence Architecture".

4. To assess and examine all aspects of the strategic issues facing your organization and your current organization-wide Strategic Plan status, as a way to understand the Reinventing Strategic Planning model, and to determine where we stand in our current strategic planning efforts.

P.M. Main Purpose: Organizing, Assessing, and Tailoring

5. To conduct an actual Plan-to-Plan session in order to determine the next steps (if any) to achieve a tailored strategic planning process for your organization (and the rest of the Strategic Management System).

6. To decide how and when to conduct an organization-wide Current State Assessment using our copyrighted "Building on Baldrige" online assessment tool.

Attendees

The Core Planning Team (including all senior management) as a minimum. It can also include other key stakeholders in the morning session as well (Executive Briefing section).

1420 Monitor Road • San Diego • California • 92110-1545 • (619) 275-6528 • Fax (619) 275-0324

EXECUTIVE BRIEFING ON
THE ABCs OF STRATEGIC MANAGEMENT™

AGENDA FOR ONE-DAY PLAN-TO-PLAN

8:30 a.m. 1. • Welcome; introductions; meeting purposes; three goals; "Wants"
  • "To Do List"; norms; materials sample plans
  • Strategic Issues list

2. What is Strategic Planning (4 choices)

3. Three main premises:
  a. "Systems Thinking—Focus on Outcomes Serving the Customer"
   — What is a system?
   — A–B–C–D–E: A New Orientation to Life
   — Four phases/many uses
   — Overview of concepts and research results
   — Strategic Planning leads the way (A–B–C–D–E)
   — Model; steps; tough choices
   — Culture change: 3 kinds of change
   — Innovation as a way to implement the Plan through Teams
   — Change via an "Organization as a System" model (or Business Excellence Architecture)
   — Right Answer #3: Customer Focus (Key Commandments)

10:00 a.m.   b. Planning is a part of management.
   — Five functions of management?
   — Right Answer #1: Strategic Management System (SMS)
   — Strategic Change Steering Committee (to manage change)
  c. "People support what they help create."
   — $E_i = f (Q \times A)$
   — Cascade of planning
   — Parallel process/key stakeholders listed
   — Right Answer #2: Leadership/Management

12:00 p.m. 4. Summary close
  Lunch

1:00 p.m. 5. Begin to conduct an actual Plan-to-Plan session
  a. Barriers and issues
  b. Amount of team building/leadership development desired
  c. Environmental Scanning
  d. Committee membership; roles; commitment
  e. Support team membership; roles; commitment

6. a. Outputs tailored to your organization
  b. Tasks; flow; timing vs. budgets
  c. Current State Assessment conducted ("Building on Baldrige") when?

4:30 p.m. 7. Next steps; "To Do List"; closure

EBRSP-Cover.pmd

1420 Monitor Road • San Diego • California • 92110-1545 • (619) 275-6528 • Fax (619) 275-0324

STRATEGIC PLANNING DEFINED

Is it:

1. An event?

2. A process?

3. A change in our roles?

4. A change in the way we run the business day-to-day?

What's your belief? Why?

STRATEGIC PLANNING IS ABOUT
MAKING TOUGH CHOICES

If Strategic Planning is going smoothly,

we're doing something wrong

(unless we have infinite resources).

EBRSP-Cover.pmd

1420 Monitor Road • San Diego • California • 92110-1545 • (619) 275-6528 • Fax (619) 275-0324

THE ABCs OF
STRATEGIC MANAGEMENT™
(Planning - People - Leadership - Change)

DEFINITION:

Strategic Planning

Plus

Strategic (Enterprise-Wide) Change

Plus

Leadership and Management

THREE GOALS:

Work On The Enterprise:
#1   Design Clarity of Purpose
      (Strategic, Business, and Annual Plans)

Work In The Enterprise:
#2   Build Simplicity of Execution
      (Successful Implementation and Enterprise-Wide Change)

Check On The Enterprise:
#3   Sustain a System of Results
      (Annual Strategic Review and Update)

The Results:
      Business Excellence and Superior Results
      (Year After Year)

THREE MAIN PREMISES:

#1   Planning and Change are *the Primary* job of Leadership

#2   "People Support What They Help Create"

#3   Use Systems Thinking
      Focus on Outcomes – Serve the Customer

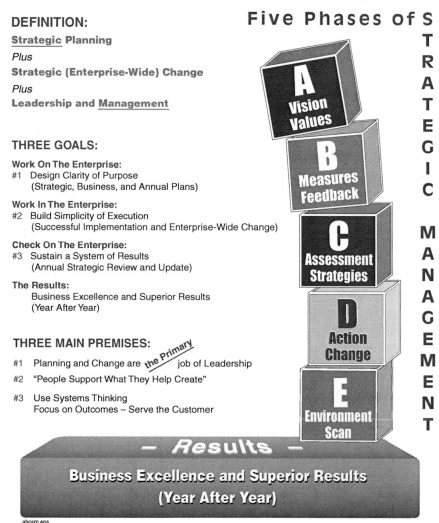

Five Phases of STRATEGIC MANAGEMENT

A Vision Values

B Measures Feedback

C Assessment Strategies

D Action Change

E Environment Scan

– Results –

Business Excellence and Superior Results
(Year After Year)

abcsm.eps

EBRSP-Cover.pmd

1420 Monitor Road • San Diego • California • 92110-1545 • (619) 275-6528 • Fax (619) 275-0324

YOUR WANTS – LEARNINGS

CRITICAL ISSUES LIST

What are the 5-10 most important critical/strategic issues facing you today as an organization, in your personal case?

1.

2.

3.

4.

5.

Note: Use this list as the content framework and "grounding" for the strategic planning process. Bring it out at the end of the planning process to ensure you've covered these issues adequately.

EBRSP-Cover.pmd

1420 Monitor Road • San Diego • California • 92110-1545 • (619) 275-6528 • Fax (619) 275-0324

STEP #1

PART A
"THE EDUCATING, ORGANIZING, ASSESSING, AND TAILORING" DAY

CONTENT: PLANNING AND CHANGE

Premise #1

"Planning and Change are *the primary* parts

of

Leadership and Management."

In fact, in today's continually changing global economy, they are the primary skills and duties of leaders.

They are the fundamentals of management; not the fads!

1420 Monitor Road • San Diego • California • 92110-1545 • (619) 275-6528 • Fax (619) 275-0324

THE SECRET OF CONSTANT GROWTH

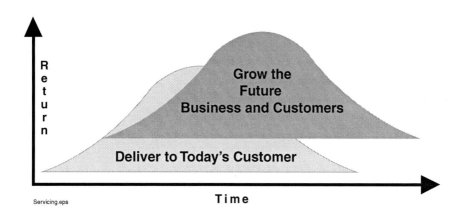

If you always do
what you've always done
you'll always get
what you've always gotten.

Insanity . . .
is doing the same things
in the same way
and expecting different results.

—*Stephen G. Haines, 1991*

1420 Monitor Road • San Diego • California • 92110-1545 • (619) 275-6528 • Fax (619) 275-0324

Why Thinking Matters

The way you think creates the results you get. The most powerful way to impact the quality of your results is to improve the ways you think.

How you think
is how you act ...
is how you are!

And determines
the results you get!

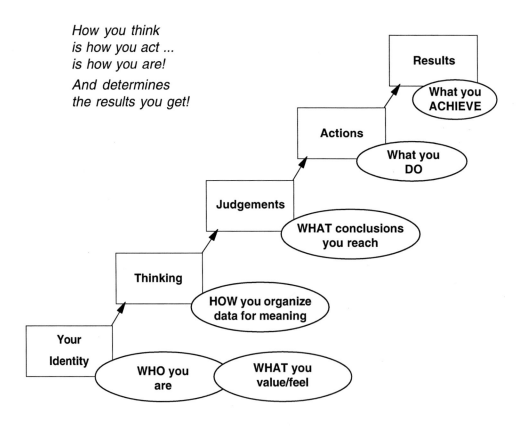

1420 Monitor Road • San Diego • California • 92110-1545 • (619) 275-6528 • Fax (619) 275-0324

Designing, Building and Sustaining
a
"Customer-Focused
High-Performance Organization"

Requires a balance in how organizations spend their time and energy between:

1. **Content**/tasks/goals and focus of the plan/business;

2. **Processes** and "how" we go about our behaviors while working on the tasks;

3. The **structures** (or context/arrangements/infra-structures) within which the *content* and *process* operate.

Content (Plan)　　　　　　　　　　**(Change) Processes**

Infra-Structures (Systems Thinking)

Content Myopia
is
Our failure to focus on processes and structures.
– yet –
Successful planning and change is dependent
on processes and structures.
This requires persistence, disciplined persistence!

EBRSP-0.pmd

1420 Monitor Road • San Diego • California • 92110-1545 • (619) 275-6528 • Fax (619) 275-0324

ANALYTIC VS. SYSTEMS THINKING
(Strategic Consistency yet Operational Flexibility)

(Outside – In – Outside Again: Both Are Then Useful)

○━━▪ Success Key: *Organizational Systems Fit, Alignment, and Integrity*

Analytic Thinking (Analysis of Today)	vs.	Systems Thinking (Synthesis for the Future)
1. We/they	vs.	1. Customers/stakeholders
2. Independent	vs.	2. Interdependent
3. Activities/tasks/means	and	3. Outcomes/ends
4. Problem solving	and	4. Solution seeking
5. Today is fine	vs.	5. Shared vision of future
6. Units/departments	and	6. Total organization
7. Silo mentality	vs.	7. Cross-functional teamwork
8. Closed environment	vs.	8. Openness and feedback
9. Department goals	and	9. Shared core strategies
10. Strategic Planning project	vs. and	10. Strategic Management System
11. Hierarchy and controls		11. Serve the customer
12. Not my job	vs.	12. Communications and collaboration
13. Isolated change	vs.	13. Systemic change
14. Linear/begin-end	vs.	14. Circular/repeat cycles
15. Little picture/view	vs.	15. Big picture/holistic perspective
16. Short-term	and	16. Long-term
17. Separate issues	vs.	17. Related issues
18. Symptoms	and	18. Root causes
19. Isolated Events	and	19. Patterns/trends
20. Activities/Actions	and	20. Clear outcome expectations (Goals/Values)
Sum: Parts are Primary	vs.	**Whole is Primary**

 Using "Analytic Approaches to Systems Problems"

Systems vs. Analytic Thinking

In Systems Thinking —the whole is primary and the parts are secondary

vs.

In Analytic Thinking—the parts are primary and the whole is secondary.

EBRSP-0.pmd

1420 Monitor Road • San Diego • California • 92110-1545 • (619) 275-6528 • Fax (619) 275-0324

A SYSTEM OF MANAGEMENT

Systems Thinking...is finding patterns and relationships, and learning to reinforce or change these patterns to fulfill your vision and mission.

DEFINITIONS AND DIFFERENCES

1.   What is management? What are its 5 functions?

   a.

   b.

   c.

   d.

   e

Our Belief

The Systems Thinking Approach™ is an absolute necessity to make sense of and succeed in today's complex world.

If life on earth is governed by the natural laws of living systems, then a successful participant should learn the concepts and principles.

—Stephen G. Haines, 1998

1420 Monitor Road • San Diego • California • 92110-1545 • (619) 275-6528 • Fax (619) 275-0324

Premise #3

"Focus on Outcomes = Serve the Customer"

Levels of Thinking

"Problems that are created by our current level of thinking

can't be solved by that same level of thinking."

—*Albert Einstein*

"So get in a helicopter with me and climb to a higher

2000 foot level and better vantage point."

—*Stephen G. Haines*

DEFINITIONS AND DIFFERENCES

1. What is a system? Draw/describe any system.
   (What are five key components?)

—Draw Here—

TWO MENTAL MAPS: WHERE TO START?

Which is it for you?

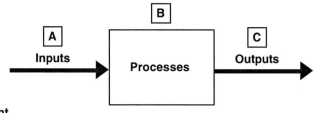

Left to Right

----------------------- *or* -----------------------

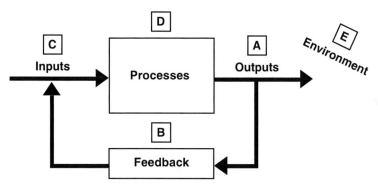

Right to Left

Why?

1420 Monitor Road • San Diego • California • 92110-1545 • (619) 275-6528 • Fax (619) 275-0324

THE SYSTEMS THINKING APPROACH™
"The Natural Way the World Works"

"A New Orientation to Life" – Our Core Technology
STRATEGIC THINKING
"From Complexity to Simplicity"

Systems: Systems are made up of a set of components that work together for the overall objective of the whole (output).

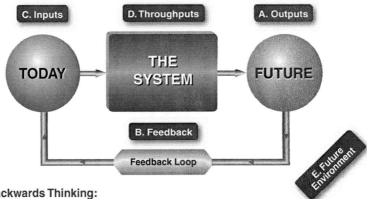

Backwards Thinking:
Five Strategic Thinking Questions – In Sequence:

A Where do we want to be? (i.e., our ends, outcomes, purposes, goals, holistic vision)

B How will we know when we get there? (i.e., the customers' needs and wants connected into a quantifiable feedback system)

C Where are we now? (i.e., today's issues and problems)

D How do we get there? (i.e., close the gap from C → A in a complete, holistic way)

E Ongoing:
What will/may change in your environment in the future?

vs. Analytic Thinking Which:

1 Starts with today and the current state, issues, and problems

2 Breaks the issues and/or problems into their smallest components

3 Solves each component separately (i.e., maximizes the solution)

4 Has no far-reaching vision or goal (just the absence of a problem)

NOTE: In Systems Thinking, the whole is primary and the parts are secondary (not vice-versa).

"If you don't know where you're going, any road will get you there."

Why Thinking Matters
"How you think... is how you act... is how you are."

MSST-02_2

EBRSP-0.pmd

1420 Monitor Road • San Diego • California • 92110-1545 • (619) 275-6528 • Fax (619) 275-0324

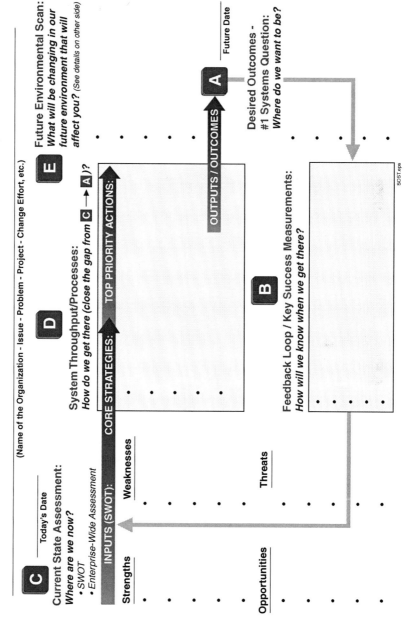

STRATEGIC THINKING – ABCs TEMPLATE
"The Science of Systems Thinking"

Desired Outcome – "Clarify and Simplify Your Thinking" – About Your Project

(Name of the Organization - Issue - Problem - Project - Change Effort, etc.)

E Future Environmental Scan:
What will be changing in our future environment that will affect you? (See details on other side)

A Desired Outcomes -
#1 Systems Question:
Where do we want to be?

Future Date

OUTPUTS / OUTCOMES

D System Throughput/Processes:
How do we get there (close the gap from C → A)?

TOP PRIORITY ACTIONS:

CORE STRATEGIES:

B Feedback Loop / Key Success Measurements:
How will we know when we get there?

C Today's Date
Current State Assessment:
Where are we now?
• SWOT
• Enterprise-Wide Assessment

INPUTS (SWOT):

Strengths

Weaknesses

Opportunities

Threats

SCST.eps

EBRSP-0.pmd

1420 Monitor Road • San Diego • California • 92110-1545 • (619) 275-6528 • Fax (619) 275-0324

STRATEGIC THINKING FRAMEWORK: SIMPLICITY

MANY USES OF THE FIVE PHASES OF THE SYSTEMS THINKING APPROACH™

Five Phases of Systems Thinking:

[A] "Creating Your Ideal Future" (Output)

[B] "Measurements of Success" (Feedback Loop)

[C] "Converting Strategies to Operations" (The Input to Action)

[D] "Successful Implementation" (Throughput/Actions)

Plus [E] Environmental Scanning (ongoing)

Uses:

1. **Comprehensive Strategic Plan**: To do a comprehensive strategic planning process for an entire organization —10-16 days offsite; full steps 1-9, yet tailored to the organization

2. **Strategic Planning Quick**: To conduct a shortened and less comprehensive version of strategic planning for an entire organization — 5 days offsite; skip KSMs

3. **Business/Functional Strategic Planning**: To conduct a shortened 3-year business planning process for a line business unit or major support function/section/program (i.e., element of the larger organization) — 5-10 days, depending on if #1 above is first accomplished

4. **Micro Strategic Planning**: To develop a strategic plan for a small organization or business — 2 days offsite; do the rest without meetings

5. **Strategic Change**: To develop an overall plan for a major project/task force (i.e., TQM, service, business process reengineering, empowerment, partnerships and teamwork, technology, etc.)

6. **Strategic Life Plan**: To conduct a personal (person, family, couple) life plan.

7. **Creating Customer Value**: To create improved value delivered to your customers.

8. **Strategic Human Resource Management**: To create "the *people edge*" in your organization.

9. **Leadership Development System**: To enhance your leadership roles and competencies as a competitive business edge.

10. **Organizational Systems Model**: To systematically implement any change effort and increase your probability of success dramatically.

11. **Team Effectiveness**: To comprehensively focus on all aspects of teams to dramatically enhance their outcomes and effectiveness.

12. **Creating the Learning Organization:** Through the Systems Thinking framework and concepts, including environmental scanning, regular feedback and clarity of outcomes.

EBRSP-0.pmd

1420 Monitor Road • San Diego • California • 92110-1545 • (619) 275-6528 • Fax (619) 275-0324

Many Powerful Centre Applications

(Of Our Ⓐ Ⓑ Ⓒ Core Systems Thinking Technology)

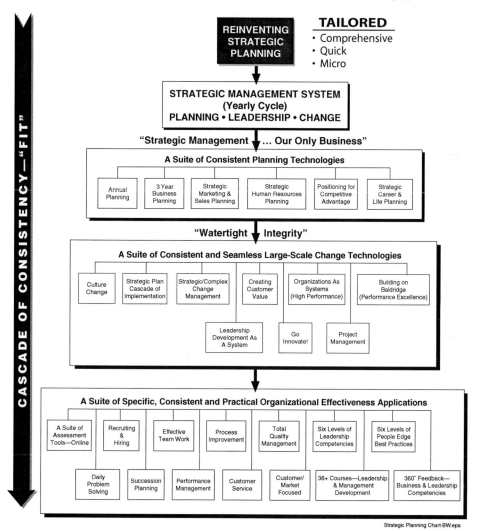

Strategic Planning Chart-BW.eps

All based on one holistic and seamless construct: The Systems Thinking Approach™

EBRSP-0.pmd

1420 Monitor Road • San Diego • California • 92110-1545 • (619) 275-6528 • Fax (619) 275-0324

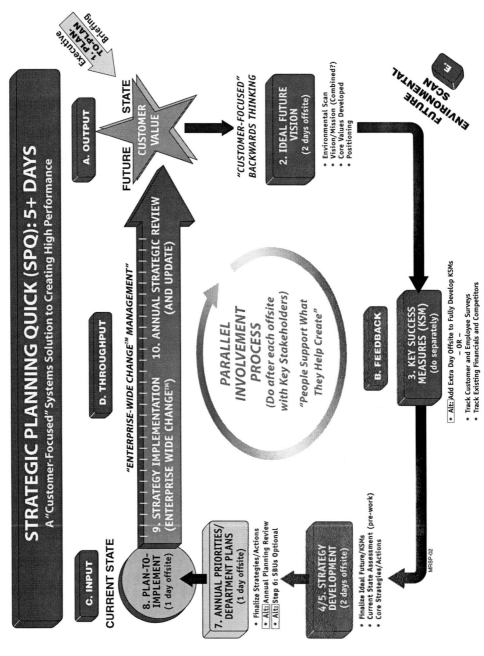

STRATEGIC PLANNING QUICK (SPQ): 5+ DAYS
A "Customer-Focused" Systems Solution to Creating High Performance

1. PLAN-TO-PLAN Executive Briefing

A. OUTPUT

FUTURE STATE

CUSTOMER VALUE

"CUSTOMER-FOCUSED" BACKWARDS THINKING

2. IDEAL FUTURE VISION (2 days offsite)
- Environmental Scan
- Vision/Mission (Combined?)
- Core Values Developed
- Positioning

FUTURE ENVIRONMENTAL SCAN E.

"ENTERPRISE-WIDE CHANGE™ MANAGEMENT"

D. THROUGHPUT

10. ANNUAL STRATEGIC REVIEW (AND UPDATE)

PARALLEL INVOLVEMENT PROCESS
(Do after each offsite with Key Stakeholders)

"People Support What They Help Create"

B. FEEDBACK

3. KEY SUCCESS MEASURES (KSM) (do separately)
- **Alt:** Add Extra Day Offsite to Fully Develop KSMs
  – OR –
- Track Customer and Employee Surveys
- Track Existing Financials and Competitors

9. STRATEGY IMPLEMENTATION (ENTERPRISE WIDE CHANGE™)

C. INPUT

CURRENT STATE

8. PLAN-TO-IMPLEMENT (1 day offsite)

7. ANNUAL PRIORITIES/ DEPARTMENT PLANS (1 day offsite)
- Finalize Strategies/Actions
- **Alt:** Annual Planning Review
- **Alt:** Step 6: SBUs Optional

4/5: STRATEGY DEVELOPMENT (2 days offsite)
- Finalize Ideal Future/KSMs
- Current State Assessment (pre-work)
- Core Strategies/Actions

MRSP-02

EBRSP-0.pmd

1420 Monitor Road • San Diego • California • 92110-1545 • (619) 275-6528 • Fax (619) 275-0324

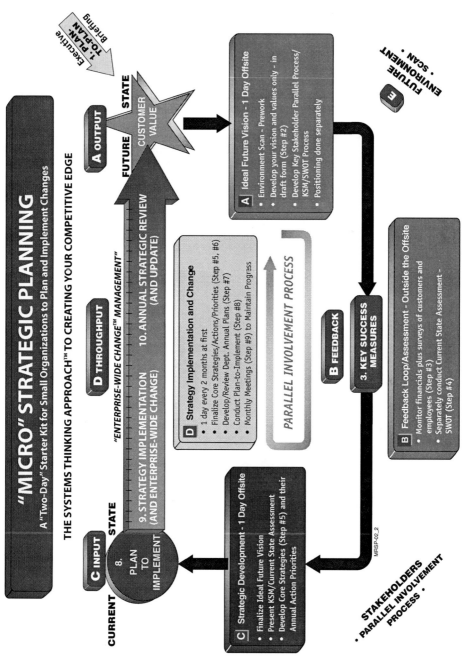

"MICRO" STRATEGIC PLANNING

A "Two-Day" Starter Kit for Small Organizations to Plan and Implement Changes

THE SYSTEMS THINKING APPROACH™ TO CREATING YOUR COMPETITIVE EDGE

1. PLAN-TO-PLAN Executive Briefing

A OUTPUT

FUTURE STATE

CUSTOMER VALUE

FUTURE ENVIRONMENT SCAN

A Ideal Future Vision - 1 Day Offsite
- Environment Scan - Prework
- Develop your vision and values only - in draft form (Step #2)
- Develop Key Stakeholder Parallel Process/ KSM/SWOT Process
- Positioning done separately

D THROUGHPUT

"ENTERPRISE-WIDE CHANGE™ MANAGEMENT"

10. ANNUAL STRATEGIC REVIEW (AND UPDATE)

D Strategy Implementation and Change
- 1 day every 2 months at first
- Finalize Core Strategies/Actions/Priorities (Step #5, #6)
- Develop/Review Dept. Annual Plans (Step #7)
- Conduct Plan-to-Implement (Step #8)
- Monthly Meetings (Step #9) to Maintain Progress

PARALLEL INVOLVEMENT PROCESS

B FEEDBACK

3. KEY SUCCESS MEASURES

B Feedback Loop/Assessment - Outside the Offsite
- Monitor financials plus surveys of customers and employees (Step #3)
- Separately conduct Current State Assessment - SWOT (Step #4)

9. STRATEGY IMPLEMENTATION (AND ENTERPRISE-WIDE CHANGE)

C INPUT

CURRENT STATE

8. PLAN TO IMPLEMENT

C Strategic Development - 1 Day Offsite
- Finalize Ideal Future Vision
- Present KSM/Current State Assessment
- Develop Core Strategies (Step #5) and their Annual Action Priorities

STAKEHOLDERS • PARALLEL INVOLVEMENT PROCESS •

MRSP-02_2

EBRSP-0.pmd

1420 Monitor Road • San Diego • California • 92110-1545 • (619) 275-6528 • Fax (619) 275-0324

STRATEGIC MANAGEMENT SYSTEM

The #2 Corporate-Wide Core Competency
required of all successful organizations!

In Summary: Organizations need a *Systems Thinking Approach* to a **Strategic Management System** with a **Yearly Cycle** in order to become a High-Performance Organization (not just a Budgeting Cycle).

Yearly Strategic Management Cycle

Strategic Management System Definition:

- A comprehensive "system" to lead, manage and change one's total organization in a conscious, well-planned, integrated fashion based on our core strategies—and using *proven research that works*—to develop and successfully achieve one's ideal future vision.

- *A new way to run a business*—i.e., "We manage our business in a systematic way based on our core strategies."

- An interactive and parti cipative method.

    "People support what they help create" – a basic truism.

- Is managed as a complete "Systems Change."
  (with strategic/annual/individual plans, budgets and measurements).

It is successful if it is:
1. Vision inspired and shared
2. Mission/customer-focused
3. Values/culturally based
4. Strategically driven
5. Outcome/results oriented

Its hallmark is *"Strategic Consistency, Operational Flexibility, and "Focus – Focus – Focus"*

"We Now Need a Strategic Management System"

I need to stress, at this point, that an effective management system is more than just the sum of the parts...it is a set of integrated policies, practices and behaviors.

Sometimes having a good management system is confused with having high-quality employees. This is a mistake—the two are quite different in some important ways: having high-quality employees does not assure an organization of having a sustainable competitive advantage or even a short-term advantage."

—Edward J. Lawler III
The Ultimate Advantage:
Creating the High-Involvement Organization

A Strategic Management System
The imperative for survival!

1420 Monitor Road • San Diego • California • 92110-1545 • (619) 275-6528 • Fax (619) 275-0324

THE CASCADE OF PLANNING™
The Systems Thinking Approach™

"STRATEGIC CONSISTENCY AND OPERATIONAL FLEXIBILITY"

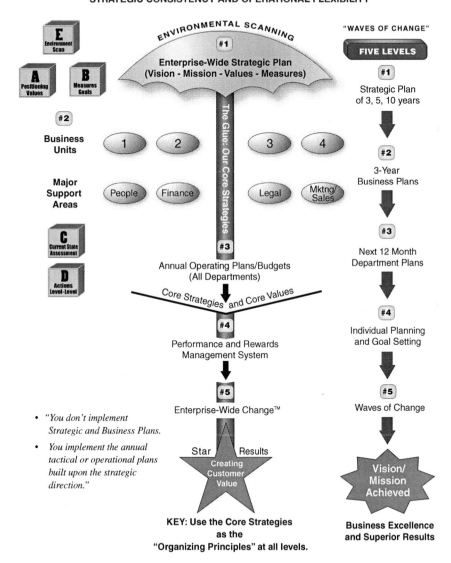

- *"You don't implement Strategic and Business Plans.*
- *You implement the annual tactical or operational plans built upon the strategic direction."*

KEY: Use the Core Strategies as the "Organizing Principles" at all levels.

Business Excellence and Superior Results

EBRSP-0.pmd

1420 Monitor Road • San Diego • California • 92110-1545 • (619) 275-6528 • Fax (619) 275-0324

BIG THREE ENTERPRISE-WIDE FAILURE ISSUES:

"Guarantee of Failure Up Front"

#1. Analytic and Piecemeal Approach to a System's Problem

- Involving multiple mindsets, frameworks, consultants and fads/silver bullets
- Instead of a *Systems Thinking Approach* and insisting on *Watertight Integrity*

#2. Mainly Focusing on an Economic Alignment of Delivery

- Involving a primary focus on productivity, processes, and bottom-line efficiencies
- Instead of combining this with "cultural attunement" issues below

#3. Mainly Focusing on Cultural Attunement and Involvement with People

- Involving a primary focus on egalitarian, participative, democratic, people processes
- Instead of combining this approach and #2 above (economic alignment)

vs.

"A Totally Integrated Systems Solution™":

- An *Enterprise-Wide Systems Thinking Approach* to Business Excellence – with a *Quadruple Bottom Line* measurement system (economics–employees–customers–society)
- *That dramatically increases Superior Results:* (Profits–Growth–Culture–Sustainability)

EBRSP-0.pmd

1420 Monitor Road • San Diego • California • 92110-1545 • (619) 275-6528 • Fax (619) 275-0324

REQUIRED ORGANIZATIONAL CAPACITY

(FOR SUCCESS IN ENTERPRISE-WIDE CHANGE™)

1. **Demonstrated Long-Term Commitment – at all levels**

2. **Effective Organizational Change Processes** to facilitate successful outcomes.

3. **Effective Organizational Change Infrastructures** in place.

4. **High Level Individual Competencies** to lead Enterprise-Wide Change™ effectively.

5. **Adequate Change Resources** devoted exclusively to Enterprise-Wide Change™.

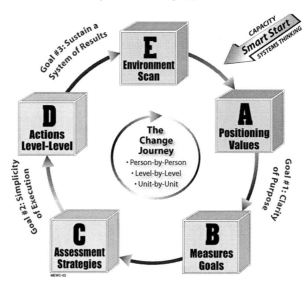

Result:
Business Excellence and Superior Results!

EBRSP-0.pmd

1420 Monitor Road • San Diego • California • 92110-1545 • (619) 275-6528 • Fax (619) 275-0324

20 COMMON MISTAKES IN STRATEGIC MANAGEMENT

Which of these mistakes are you making? Score this 1-5 (H= 5, yes, all or most of the time; M = 3, yes, at times we do; L = 1, no, we don't make this mistake):

_____ 1. Failing to integrate planning at all levels

_____ 2. Keeping planning separate from day-to-day management

_____ 3. Conducting long-range forecasting only, with extrapolations from the past

_____ 4. Having a piecemeal & separate approach to strategic planning and strategic change

_____ 5. Developing vision, mission, and value statements only/with no effective measures

_____ 6. Having yearly weekend retreats and annual near-term thinking only

_____ 7. Failing to complete an effective implementation process

_____ 8. Violating the "people support what they help create" involvement premise, and best practice

_____ 9. Conducting business as usual after doing strategic planning - The SPOTS Syndrome (Strategic Plan on Top Shelf gathering dust)

_____ 10. Failing to make the "tough choices" or suppression of differences of opinions

_____ 11. Lacking a Quadruple Bottom Line, Balanced Scoreboard; measuring activities, not what's important results & success

_____ 12. Failing to define and/or plan for Strategic Business Units And Functional Departments in a meaningful way

_____ 13. Neglecting to benchmark yourself against the competition & Best Practices

_____ 14. Seeing the planning document as an end in itself - missing the need for a yearly Strategic Management System & Cycle

_____ 15. Having confusing terminology, language, and a Bureaucratic Annual Process

_____ 16. Trying to facilitate the process yourself by being penny wise and pound foolish when it comes to the use of a master consultant/facilitator

_____ 17. Failing to identify, develop, and defend your unique positioning in the marketplace vs. the competition in the eyes of the customer

_____ 18. Failing to adequately involve the CEO, and top management as active leaders of this key process

_____ 19. Isolating yourself from the competitive environment and a failure to do meaningful and regular quarterly environmental scanning

_____ 20. Form and ritual rather than substance

Total # of H x 5 = _____ + M x 3 = _____ + L x 1= _____ = _____(Total Score)

Out of a Possible Score of 100 Pts.
80 – 100 = Strategic Management is a visionary art for your senior leadership
60 – 79 = Strategic Management is a serious effort for your organization
40 – 59 = Strategic Management is not understood or appreciated
20 – 39 = Strategic Management is bankrupt - what are the potential consequences?

EBRSP-0.pmd

1420 Monitor Road • San Diego • California • 92110-1545 • (619) 275-6528 • Fax (619) 275-0324

15 KEY BENEFITS OF A STRATEGIC MANAGEMENT SYSTEM

Which of these benefits are still missing in your organization?

_____ 1. Taking an organization-wide, proactive approach to a changing global world.

_____ 2. Building an executive team that serves as a model of cross-functional or horizontal teamwork.

_____ 3. Having an intense executive development and strategic orientation process.

_____ 4. Defining focused, quantifiable outcome measures of success.

_____ 5. Making intelligent budgeting decisions.

_____ 6. Clarifying your competitive advantage.

_____ 7. Reducing conflict; empowering the organization.

_____ 8. Providing clear guidelines for day-to-day decision making.

_____ 9. Creating a critical mass for change.

_____10. "Singing from the same hymnal" throughout the organization.

_____11. Clarifying and simplifying the barrage of management techniques.

_____12. Empowering middle managers.

_____13. Focusing everyone in the organization on the same overall framework.

_____14. Speeding up implementation of the core strategies.

_____15. Providing tangible tools for dealing with the stress of change.

EBRSP-0.pmd

1420 Monitor Road • San Diego • California • 92110-1545 • (619) 275-6528 • Fax (619) 275-0324

– SUMMARY –
SYSTEMS THINKING—A NEW WAY TO THINK

Start Thinking More About:

1. The Environment   **E**   (and opportunities)

2. The Outcomes   **A**   (and results)

3. The Future   **A**   (and direction)

4. The Feedback   **B**   (and learning)

5. The Goals   **B**   (and measures)

6. The Whole Organization   **D**   (and helicopters @ 5,000 feet)

7. The Relationships   **D**   (and patterns/leverage points)

8. The Fit   **D**   (and synergy of multiple change projects)

Think Less About **C** so much:

1. Today's Issues and Problems
2. Parts and Events
3. Boxes/Silos
4. Single Activities of Change
5. Defensiveness
6. Inputs and Resources
7. Separateness
8. Maximizing Pieces

How we think ... is how we act ... is how we are!

EBRSP-0.pmd

1420 Monitor Road • San Diego • California • 92110-1545 • (619) 275-6528 • Fax (619) 275-0324

Potential Plan-to-Plan Tasks
to
Educate, Assess, Tailor, and Organize the process to your needs.

EDUCATE

1. Organization Specification Sheet

2. Executive Briefing on Strategic Planning

3. Organizational Fact Sheet for Strategic Planning

4. Individual Commitment to Strategic Management Must Be High (not just to Strategic Planning)

5. Organizational Commitment to a Strategic Management System/Yearly Cycle (Planning-Leadership-Change)

ORGANIZE

1. Strategic Planning "Staff Support Team" Needed

2. Identification of Key Stakeholders

3. Planning Team Membership Selected

4. Key Stakeholder Involvement

5. Strategic Planning Meeting (Process Observer for Team Building)

6. Action/"To Do" List, Minutes (Format to use)

7. Meeting Processing (Guide to Use)

8. Meeting Closure—Action Planning Checklist (at the end of each meeting)

ASSESS

1. A High-Performance Best Practices Organizational Assessment (*Building on Baldrige)*

2. Pre-work Strategic Planning Briefing Questionnaire

3. Personal Readiness/Experiences in Strategic Planning

4. Strategic Planning Process (past Levels of Effectiveness/Simplicity Audit)

5. Readiness Steps and Actions (Barriers and Issues)

6. Critical Issues List

7. Initial Environmental Scanning required

TAILOR

1. Tailored to Your Needs: of the Reinventing Strategic Planning Model

2. Strategic Planning Links: (to Annual Budgets Dept. Plans/SBUs/COBs)

3. Leadership Development Skills (Organizational and Individual Self-Change/Training Needed)

4. Strategic Planning Updates Communicated to Others

5. Learning possibilities during Strategic Planning

6. Enterprise-Wide Change Process: Smart Start and Plan-to-Plan Implement Scheduled

EBRSP-1.pmd

1420 Monitor Road • San Diego • California • 92110-1545 • (619) 275-6528 • Fax (619) 275-0324

THE PLAYERS OF CHANGE

Enterprise-Wide Change™:
The Systems Thinking Approach™

MBPC-01_2

The Multi-Year Cascade of Change Journey:
Person-by-Person ◆ Level-by-Level ◆ Unit-by-Unit

1420 Monitor Road • San Diego • California • 92110-1545 • (619) 275-6528 • Fax (619) 275-0324

PLANNING TEAM MEMBERSHIP

CRITERIA FOR THE CORE PLANNING TEAM SELECTION

Organization-Wide vs. Narrow Perspective?

- Each core planning team participant must be willing to have an organization-wide perspective and orientation in order to be on the planning team. Status quo, narrow perspectives and interests, or *representing only parts of the organization* must be left *at the door* in order for strategic planning to be successful.

- Strategic planning is not a collection of special interest groups coming together but individuals willing to look at the "Gestalt" or whole organization as it interacts in its dynamic environment.

- An openness to future change is a key requirement for success, as is a focus on the customer and the environment.

- Later, at the end of the process, *adding* a narrower or functional perspective is appropriate...in order to implement the strategic plan through annual, department, and individual work plans.

#1 Core Planning Team Composition
- Sense of clear direction
- Ownership and commitment — senior level/middle management
- Data reality — key players
- Stakeholders — key to broad perspective
- Helps implementation — key players
- Staff support team
- Leader preference/comfort

#2 Numbers Vs. Group Dynamics Reasonableness
A. 6-8 people = best size for group dynamics/team building
B. 10-15 people = okay size (2-3 subgroups)
C. 16+ people = a "mess" — crowd control becomes the issue

#3 Involvement of Others Through Parallel Process
- Through data collection homework at Current State Assessment step
- Through involvement in business/annual department planning
- Through asking their opinions/reactions to drafts (2-4 times throughout the process)

EBRSP-1.pmd

1420 Monitor Road • San Diego • California • 92110-1545 • (619) 275-6528 • Fax (619) 275-0324

STRATEGIC PLANNING "STAFF SUPPORT TEAM"

List Staff Support Team Names:

Position	Typical Tasks	Name
1. Planning	• Strategic/Annual Planning • Business Planning • Current State Assessment	
2. Finance	• Key Sucess Measure Coordinator • Budgeting • Current State Assessment	
3. Human Resources	• Performance/Rewards Management • Training and Development	
4. Communications	• Updates After Each Meeting • Print Final Plan/Plaques • Rollout Plan	
5. Administrative Assistant	• Logistics/Follow-up • Laptop Mintues/Document Revisions • Drafts Strategic Plan	
6. Internal Coordinator **Coordinates** or does 1-7 themselves	**Minimum List** • Parallel Process • Internal Facilitator • Coordinates Entire Process • Facilitates SCLSC • Teach Organization About This	
7. External Consultant (Your Partner in Strategic Management)	• Facilitates Planning/Change Steering Committee & Project Teams • Develops Internal Coordinator • Devil's Advocate/Tough Choices • Advisor on all Planning/Leadership/ Change Efforts • Year-Long Advisor and Partner to CEO/Senior Management	

EBRSP-1.pmd

1420 Monitor Road • San Diego • California • 92110-1545 • (619) 275-6528 • Fax (619) 275-0324

THE EXTERNAL ROLE OF A STRATEGIC PLANNING FACILITATOR

1. Acts as a "devil's advocate" by posing frank questions on:
   - following your values in the strategic planning process.
   - pushing for concrete decisions, directions, and priorities.
   - helping you do what you've said you want to achieve in strategic planning (i.e., narrow our focus; look for a future vision that involves change, etc.).
   - challenging you and your key people about the issues you are backing away from; not doing what you said you want to achieve; making the hard decisions.
   - moving from Vision to Reality.

2. Constantly crafts and facilitates the planning process with you, but lets you determine the direction of the plan, your future, and the planning process itself.

3. Brings expertise—content/technical and process facilitation – with objectivity.

4. Assists your internal staff support team in:
   - being a teacher to line managers/executives.
   - communicating with the rest of the organization about plans. (Assist executives to do this regularly.)
   - using people to plan, not computers. Computers are just a tool.
   - developing the knowledge and skills to eventually carry out the planning and implementation process yourself.

5. Facilitates your Strategic Change Management process to ensure that you build your first **Strategic Management Yearly Cycle (Corporate-Wide Core Competency #2).**

6. Assists you in developing an overall **Leadership Development System (Corporate-Wide Core Competency #1)** tied to your Strategic Management System.

7. Assists you in implementing the results of the "Building on Baldrige" Best Practices Assessment to ensure **"Watertight Integrity" to your Vision/Positioning (Corporate-Wide Core Competency #3).**

Consultant Skills in Strategic Planning: *Seven Requirements*

1. A strong business, economic, and industry orientation
2. Expertise in strategic planning and project management
3. An excellent sense of overall organization fit, functioning, and design
4. Understanding of human behavior and group/organizational dynamics
5. Knowledge/skills in large scale change and transition management
6. Consulting steps and facilitator/process/meetings management skills
7. Strong internal sense of self, ego, and self-esteem

Internal consultants should beware of the CEO who allows you to take too great a role in the strategic planning process. It places you in a perilous position and you may become the point person for change for a weak, disinterested CEO without the strength/will to take the leadership role.

EBRSP-1.pmd

1420 Monitor Road • San Diego • California • 92110-1545 • (619) 275-6528 • Fax (619) 275-0324

Premise #2

"People Support What They Help Create"
(The Parallel Involvement Process)

Participative Management

"People want input into decisions that affect them

prior to those decisions being finalized."

—*Stephen G. Haines*

Key Dialogue Points to Remember

For The Core Planning Team

- This is actually *strategic thinking*—reexamining—looking at different points of view— taking the time we should, but never do back on the job.

- Importance of the *hierarchy of ideas* and linkage of one concept/document to another to create a *strategic plan*.

- Elegant simplicity vs. lots of adjectives and words. (Rule of three; key words italicized)

- This is a search for meaning and future direction for the organization—not a position-taking exercise.

- Be careful when combining concepts together to shorten documents; explicitly emphasize what is new or currently missing in the document.

- Listen carefully to others; assimilate their ideas; search for *nuggets* ... and use *"consensus"* decision making. i.e. I can *"actively support"* the decisions.

- Know when you are dealing with a substantive issue and when you are *wordsmithing* (i.e, limit wordsmithing to useful times only—but use layman's terminology vs. your business jargon).

- Explain your position and discuss the rationale, logic, and "why" behind your position; worry less about the position itself.

- Closure/consensus is the ultimate goal—not just talking/presenting my own ideas.

EBRSP-1.pmd

1420 Monitor Road • San Diego • California • 92110-1545 • (619) 275-6528 • Fax (619) 275-0324

HEALTHY GROUND RULES

MEETING GUIDELINES FOR TEAM LEARNING AND EFFECTIVENESS

I. Participation	II. Dialogue	III. Consensus
1. **Everyone participates** with an organization-wide view *(broad, not parochial/functional)*	8. **Actively listen**; don't dominate *(one person talk at a time; no 4th of July fireworks)*	15. Use **consensus** decision making where possible *("Actively Support"; okay to state agreement, even violent agreement)*
2. **Protect** everyone's **right** to be **heard** *(minority view; show respect)*	9. Be creative and **think out of the box** *("What if")*	16. Identify and **crack the nuggets;** hang in there, even when frustrated *(difficult, complex issues)*
3. Be **hard** on the **issues** and **soft** on the **people** *(okay to disagree; don't be disagreeable)*	10. Share our **logic**, rationale and **why** underneath our opinions *(logic is key—not view)*	17. If everything is **going smoothly**, we're doing **something wrong** *(differences and conflict are normal, be persistent, hang in)*
4. **Maintain the schedule**—start/ end on time or renegotiate *(return from breaks on time)*	11. Stay on track — focus–**focus**– focus *(be personally disciplined; no monologues to the deaf)*	
5. **Limit interruptions**—phones, personal matters operational issues *(low side conversations)*	12. Have **intellectual honest with yourself** in discussions *("leave your shield at the door"; be willing to let go)*	18. Listen, dialogue and **learn; discover** the answers together *(no one has all the answers)*
6. **Listen to the skeptics**— "Skeptics are my best friends" *(they make you think; show why ideas might fail)*	13. Beware of false **"X" vs. "Y" arguments**—say "yes, both" *(no win-lose games)*	19. Spend **more time on substance** *(less wordsmithing)*
7. Being an **honest devil's advocate** is fine— *(ask why, logic, rationale to test your thinking)*	14. Focus **on one topic at a time** *(no "topic jumping", use self-discipline, be self-aware; no unbridled behaviors)*	20. Search for **common sense and future direction**: Strategic Thinking *(be willing to change your view vs. "being right" and position-taking)*
		21. Focus on/assist with **closure, agreements** *(facilitators cannot do it alone)*

IV. **And Finally, "Stop Checks"**

22. Improve our **teamwork and group effectiveness** (stop and check our progress against these; use straightforward and honest feedback; be direct in talking with each other, toughen up)

23. **Ask the #1 Systems Thinking Question**: What is our purpose/desired outcome/goal? (ask it over and over again)

EBRSP-1.pmd

1420 Monitor Road • San Diego • California • 92110-1545 • (619) 275-6528 • Fax (619) 275-0324

FIND THE 2-3 "NUGGETS"

(IN EACH STRATEGIC PLANNING PROCESS)

Characteristics

1. Important issues
2. Complex issues
3. No easy answers
4. Differences in terminology
5. Strong feelings
6. Differing views (legitimate)
7. Challenges to each other
8. Consequences for jobs/ accountability

9. Clash of values/cultures
10. Assumptions made/hidden/ threatened
11. Shifting ground rules of the industry
12. 1-2 "fringe players" of different views/perspectives
— new ideas, paradigms
13. Changing issues/point of views
— past vs. present vs. future

"Nuggets require Strategic/Systems Thinking
before planning.
Take the time to do it right!

Challenge the Obvious
If things are going smoothly
we must be doing something wrong
(unless we have infinite resources)

Question: Do we want to be polite or effective?

EBRSP-1.pmd

1420 Monitor Road • San Diego • California • 92110-1545 • (619) 275-6528 • Fax (619) 275-0324

WHO IS IN CONTROL?

The Person Talking or the Person Listening/Asking?

Answer? _____

_____

Why? _____

_____

Rule: The person asking the questions is the person in control.

Why:

1. Because we almost all respond to other's questions.
2. The questions can change and focus the topic.
3. People like to be "The Shell Answer Man" and answer your questions.
4. People often do not respond to other's statements, just to their own.

Do I Mostly Talk Or Listen?

CONFLICT: BE WILLING TO CHANGE VS. BEING RIGHT

Why is it so hard to change our point of view?

Most often it is because we are not nearly as interested in resolving the conflict and possibly creating a new pearl as we are in being right.

When we perceive conflict as a threat to our ego, our reaction is to defend or to attack. All our energy and mind-power are used in the protection of our ego, not in the growth of our being.

Fear of failure reigns supreme.

1420 Monitor Road • San Diego • California • 92110-1545 • (619) 275-6528 • Fax (619) 275-0324

DIALOGUE VS. DEBATE

—Adapted from Lily Evans

Dialogue is based on	vs.	Debate is based on
1. Asking	vs.	1. Knowing
2. Questions	vs.	2. Answers
3. Sharing	vs.	3. Winning
4. Full Participation	vs.	4. Domineering
5. Respect	vs.	5. Power
6. Exploring	vs.	6. (Re)stating
7. Listening	vs.	7. Proving

The Top 10 Secrets for Healthy, Positive and Productive Communication

1. Check your motive.
2. Get to the point.
3. Stick to the point.
4. Remember that your body speaks volumes.
5. Check your tone.
6. Say what you mean and mean what you say.
7. Listen first for understanding.
8. Practice, practice and practice.
9. Get help with tough communications.
10. Simplicity is best. Don't hide behind language.

This piece was originally submitted by Catherine and Steve Martin, Relationship Experts, who can be reached at positive-way@mail.com

STRATEGIC PLANNING PROCESS:
LEVELS OF PLANNING EFFECTIVENESS

TOWARDS A HIGH PERFORMANCE ORGANIZATION

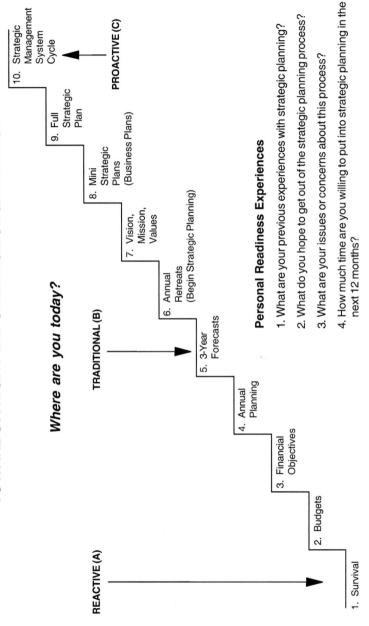

Where are you today?

REACTIVE (A)

TRADITIONAL (B)

PROACTIVE (C)

1. Survival
2. Budgets
3. Financial Objectives
4. Annual Planning
5. 3-Year Forecasts
6. Annual Retreats (Begin Strategic Planning)
7. Vision, Mission, Values
8. Mini Strategic Plans (Business Plans)
9. Full Strategic Plan
10. Strategic Management System Cycle

Personal Readiness Experiences

1. What are your previous experiences with strategic planning?

2. What do you hope to get out of the strategic planning process?

3. What are your issues or concerns about this process?

4. How much time are you willing to put into strategic planning in the next 12 months?

EBRSP-1.pmd

1420 Monitor Road • San Diego • California • 92110-1545 • (619) 275-6528 • Fax (619) 275-0324

POTENTIAL BARRIERS
IN THE STRATEGIC PLANNING PROCESS

"Skeptics are my best friends." Why?

1. Lack of senior management belief and commitment to planning, or at least to investigating Plan-to-Plan.

2. Group size too large or too small to include the "collective leadership".

3. Culture doesn't believe in, or reward, planning.

4. Time/resource commitment isn't there to plan; unrealistic expectations; too fast/rushed.

5. Day-to-day growth and pressures too dominant.

6. Adapting the Strategic Planning Model to your unique situation.

7. Lack of willingness to be visionary, proactive, and creative.

8. Tough choices avoided; failure to set priorities and focus budgets.

9. Reactive, low risk, rewards mentality; low reinforcement for strategic thinking.

10. KSMs/measuring success mentality missing.

11. Past history and mistakes in previous planning attempts.

12. Perseverance in completing the planning process itself.

13. Frequently changing priorities and focus; not persevering on one track; inconsistent decisions.

14. Bridging to and managing the implementation and change process.

15. Keeping up momentum in implementation (long-term).

16. Low commitment to the final products of the strategic plan.

17. "SPOTS syndrome" — Strategic Plan on Top Shelf; no formal implementation.

18. Failure to provide the needed resources — financial and personnel to implement.

19. Poor information on the SKEPTIC environments (Social, "K"ompetitionEconomic, Political, Technical, Industry, and Customer).

20. Differing directions, priorities among business/organizational units.

21. Conflicts, politics, lack of interpersonal skills among top management when working together.

22. Failure to view, commit to, and implement a Leadership Development System as the #1 Core Competency required for all successful organizations.

23. Failure to understand the need for this to be a core part of a Yearly Strategic Management System and Cycle (the #2 Core Competency required for all successful organizations).

EBRSP-1.pmd

EBRSP – All rights reserved.

1420 Monitor Road • San Diego • California • 92110-1545 • (619) 275-6528 • Fax (619) 275-0324

KEY STAKEHOLDER ASSESSMENT

1. Who are all our stakeholders (both Internal and External)? Be specific:

INTERNAL	EXTERNAL

2. Decide who are the top 5-7 stakeholders in terms of importance to the success(both plus and minus) of our Strategic Planning / Enterprise-Wide change process.

    Both its:

    A: Clarity of Purpose

    B: Simplicity of Execution

PARALLEL INVOLVEMENT PROCESS
"People Support What They Help Create"

INSTEAD OF D.A.D.: Decide, Announce, Defend

SET UP THE PLANNING & CHANGE COMMUNITY

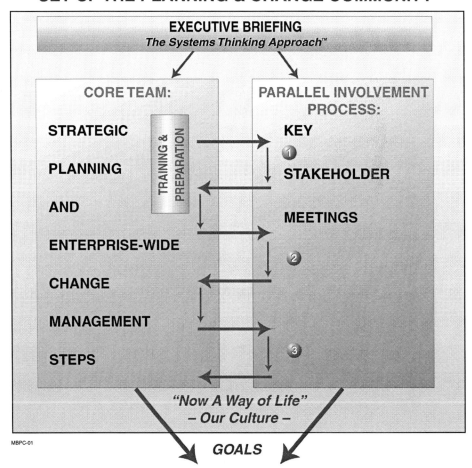

EXECUTIVE BRIEFING
The Systems Thinking Approach™

CORE TEAM:

STRATEGIC

PLANNING

AND

ENTERPRISE-WIDE

CHANGE

MANAGEMENT

STEPS

TRAINING & PREPARATION

PARALLEL INVOLVEMENT PROCESS:

KEY

①

STAKEHOLDER

MEETINGS

②

③

"Now A Way of Life"
– Our Culture –

MBPC-01

GOALS

#1 Ownership For Implementation / Execution

#2 Best Possible Decisions On Future Direction / Purpose

1420 Monitor Road • San Diego • California • 92110-1545 • (619) 275-6528 • Fax (619) 275-0324

PARALLEL INVOLVEMENT PROCESS MEETINGS

PURPOSE (AND AGENDA)

1. To explain the Strategic Planning / Enterprise-Wide Change effort and your role/involvement in it.
2. To understand the draft documents clearly.
3. To give us input and feedback to take back to the full core planning team

   - **Guarantee**: Your feedback will be seriously considered.

   - **Limitation**: Input is being gathered from many different peole. Therefore, it is impossible for each person's input to be automatically placed in the final document exactly as desired.

OVERALL MEETING PURPOSE

1. This is an **information sharing and input/feedback** meeting.
2. It is **not a decision-making meeting**. This will be done by the Core Planning/Enterprise-Wide Team at their next meeting, based on your feedback.

THE "MAGIC" IS IN THE ITERATION

How to get the best answers?

1. **Creativity and Innovation come from:**
   - intense dialogue/thought
   - time to get away/reflect—doing your day-to-day job
   - a second or even third intense dialogue
     - in the Parallel Process
     - in the next planning meeting

2. **Testing via the Parallel Involvement Process is the crucible to:**
   - improve the quality of the answers
   - develop "buy in" and commitment to the answer

The Question is—*When are you "ready" for closure?*

EBRSP-1.pmd

1420 Monitor Road • San Diego • California • 92110-1545 • (619) 275-6528 • Fax (619) 275-0324

DEVELOPING A STRATEGIC ENVIRONMENTAL SCANNING SYSTEM (SESS)

THE SIX STEPS INCLUDE THE FOLLOWING:

1. Identify the organization's Environmental Scan needs, especially for the next round of Strategic Planning (Annual Updates).

2. Generate a list of information sources that provide core inputs (i.e., trade shows, publications, technical meetings, customers, shareholders).

3. Identify those employees who will participate in the Environmental Scanning Process. (They do not have to be members of the Planning Team.)

4. Assign scanning tasks to several members of the organization.

5. Collect data on a regular basis.

6. Disseminate the information in a large group meeting:
    *   on a yearly basis and quarterly at the Strategic Change Leadership Steering Committee meeting

INITIAL ENVIRONMENTAL SCANNING REQUIRED

List the initial environmental scanning that needs to be conducted at the beginning of the strategic planning process.

What areas scanned/ data collected?	Who Responsible?	When Covered?

EBRSP-1.pmd

1420 Monitor Road • San Diego • California • 92110-1545 • (619) 275-6528 • Fax (619) 275-0324

Future Environmental SKEPTIC Scanning/Trends

List the 5-10 environmental trends - projections - opportunities - threats facing you over the life of your plan:

S — Socio-Demographics (People/Society):

K — Competition/Substitutes:

E — Economics:

E — Ecology:

P — Politica /Regulatory:

T — Technical:

I — Industry/Suppliers:

C — Customer/Citizens:

EBRSP-1.pmd

1420 Monitor Road • San Diego • California • 92110-1545 • (619) 275-6528 • Fax (619) 275-0324

WHAT IS DIFFERENT ABOUT OUR REINVENTING STRATEGIC PLANNING?

(In the 21ST Century)

21ST CENTURY ENVIRONMENTAL SCAN	NEW STRATEGIC MANAGEMENT CONCEPTS (Leadership-Planning-Change)
1. Dynamic environment	1. Importance of regular environmental scan - do first
2. Desire for clear and broader results	2. Measurement focused—"quadruple bottom line"
3. Very complex world	3. Simplicity is key—Rule of 3 of 1
4. More competitive environment/drive to commodity/price only	4. Unique Positioning is essential—the right answer does count
5. Nonlinear future environment/ major disruptions	5. Ideal Future State is the place to start – not the Current State Assessment
6. More demanding customers	6. "Data-Based Decision-Making"—planning team with an external customer orientation are key; not just senior management (support jobs)
7. More skeptical and less engaged employees	7. Parallel Process and Large-Group Annual Dept. Review Meeting—maximum involvement of rest of management/key employees
8. More diverse employee culture, background, ethnicity, age and values	8. Glue of Core Strategies and Core Values key to Cascade of Planning and implementation—with accountability of performance and rewards
9. Attention span shorter/more "noise" in the world (concept of entropy— all things run down and die)	9. Need for Monthly, Quarterly Progress Review meetings and Annual Strategic Review (and Update)—"buy in *and* stay in" are both key
10. No one has all the answers or skills— how to make sense of all the books, fads, theories?	10. Leadership Development done concurrently with Planning and Implementation to stay abreast of new concepts and assimilate the learning for us **(Core Corporate Competency #1)**
11. "Long-Term" is nothing without "shorter-term" successful implementation and change linked to longer-term	11. Create a Strategic Management System and Annual Cycle as new way to run the business **(Core Corporate Competency #2)**
12. Complexity *within* all organizations	12. Need "Strategic Business Redesign for "Watertight Integrity"—systems view, understanding and challenge of change **(Core Corporate Competency #3)**
13. Faster pace of work and life	13. Tailored Strategic Management System to your unique needs, from "Micro" to "Quick" to "Comprehensive" Strategic Planning
14. Faster pace and variety of changes	14. Flexibility and agility of implementation are key— "emergent strategies" a way of life *("Plan is a living-breathing document")*

EBRSP-1.pmd

1420 Monitor Road • San Diego • California • 92110-1545 • (619) 275-6528 • Fax (619) 275-0324

DATA-BASED DECISION-MAKING

1.   What Data/Information do you have?
2.   What do you need for better decision-making (i.e., more than just opinions, intuition and past experiences):

Topic	Data Available	Who Has It?	Data Needed	Who is Responsible?
I. Employees				
1. Satisfaction with Company Values				
2. Turnover				
3. Organization-Wide Assessment (Building on Baldrige)				
4. What Else?				
II. Customers				
5. Customer Satisfaction				
6. Customer Needs/Wants				
7. What Else?				
III. Marketing				
8. Market Segment Research				
9. Market Share Research				
10. Product Performance				
11. Competitor Analysis				
12. What Else?				
IV. Finance				
13. Balance Sheet				
14. P/L Statement				
15. ROE/ROA				
16. Cash Flow				
17. What Else?				

REINVENTING STRATEGIC PLANNING (TAILORED TO YOUR NEEDS)

Based on your current understanding of the Reinventing Strategic Planning and Enterprise-Wide Change Management Models (& Strategic Management), please list the Importance (H-M-L) of now developing each potential deliverable for your organization – * items are **"must do"** to work with the Centre as **your Partner for the next year (as a minimum).**

Strategic Planning—Steps #2-5 – Goal #1

E * 1. _____ Environmental Scanning (SKEPTIC) – in a Dynamic Environment

A 1. _____ Vision—Our Ideal Future, Aspirations, Guiding Star

2. _____ Mission—Who, What, Why We Exist

3. _____ Values—Our Guiding Principles, To Guide Organizational Behaviors

4. _____ Driving Force(s)—Positioning, Our Competitive Edge

5. _____ Rallying Cry—3-6 Key Motivational Words

B * 1. _____ Key Success Measures—Quantifiable Measures of Success cascaded down through the organizational levels for Line-of-Sight accountability.

C₁ 1. _____ Current State Assessment: SWOT plus other assessments

2. _____ Best Practices Organization-Wide Assessment - Watertight Integrity – "Building on the Baldrige" – **Corporate-Wide Core Competency #3.**

C₂ 3. _____ Core Strategies—Major Means, Approaches, Methods to Achieve Our Vision

4. _____ Actions/Yearly Priorities Under Each Core Strategy

Business Units—Step #6

5. _____ SBU/MPAs Defined—Strategic Business Units/Market Segments, or Major Program Areas

6. _____ Business/Key Support Plans—3-Year Mini Strategic Plans for Units

Annual Plans—Step #7

7. _____ Annual Plans/Priorities (Department Plans)

8. _____ Resource Allocation/Strategic Budgeting (including guidelines)

Individuals/Teams

9. _____ Individual Performance Management System—Tied to Strategic Planning

10. _____ Rewards and Recognition System—Tied to Strategic Planning

Bridge the Gap—Step #8 – Smart Start

D₁ 1. _____ Plan-to-Implement Day – Facilitated by the Centre – Get Educated, Organized and Tailor Our Enterprise-Wide Change Management Process/Structures

2. _____ Clarify and develop your Enterprise-Wide Change capabilities and resources

Enterprise-Wide Change - Steps #9-#10 – Goal #2

3. _____ Monthly Change Leadership Team meetings facilitated by the Centre

4. _____ Use Innovation as the vehicle for Change – to implement the Plan (Strategic/Project/Sponsorship Teams) and create Innovation as your Culture

EBRSP-1.pmd

1420 Monitor Road • San Diego • California • 92110-1545 • (619) 275-6528 • Fax (619) 275-0324

REINVENTING STRATEGIC PLANNING
(TAILORED TO YOUR NEEDS) *continued*

Attunement of People/Support Systems—Step #9 – Modules #3-#4-#5:		

D₂ 5a. _____ Values/Cultural Change Skills – Module #1

5b. _____ Management Change Skills/Managing Enterprise-Wide Change Skills – Module #3

5c. _____ HR Programs/Processes—Employee Development Board – Module #4

5d. _____ Employee Involvement/Participative Management Skills/Empowerment

5e. _____ Professional Mgt. & Leadership Developoment–Six Natural Levels of Leadership Competencies/Skills – **Corporate-Wide Core Competency #1** – Module #5

5f. _____ Strategic Communications: Knowledge and Skills

Teamwork:

5g. _____ Teamwork for Executive Team

5h. _____ Teamwork for Department Teams

5i. _____ Teamwork for Cross-Functional Relationships/Teams

5j. _____ Strategic Alliances

Becoming Customer-Focused – Step #9 – Module #6

6a. _____ Strategic Marketing and Sales Planning

6b. _____ Customer and Market Data/Feedback and Wants

6c. _____ Customer Service Standards and Consistency

6d. _____ New Product Development and/or Quality

6e. _____ Sales and Marketing Effectiveness

Alignment of Delivery—Step #9 – Module # 7

7a. _____ Conduct a Strategic Business Design study to check for Watertight Integrity to your Vision – **Corporate-Wide Core Competency #3**

7b. _____ Organization Structure/Redesign

7c. _____ Business Process Reengineering—to lower costs/improve response *(customer-focused)*

7d. _____ Blow-Out Bureaucracy (& Waste)

7e. _____ Information Technology—Technology Steering Group

Focus on the Vital Few ("STAR" Results) – Module #8

8a. _____ Quality Products and Services

8b. _____ Customer Service

8c. _____ Speed/Responsiveness/Convenience for the Customer

8d. _____ Choice, Fashion, Control, Customized

Yearly Update – Step #10 – Goal #3: Strategic Management Cycle

D₃ 9. _____ Annual Strategic Review and Update Process – Building our Yearly Strategic Management Cycle – **Corporate-Wide Core Competency #2**

EBRSP-1.pmd

1420 Monitor Road • San Diego • California • 92110-1545 • (619) 275-6528 • Fax (619) 275-0324

LEARNING POSSIBILITIES DURING STRATEGIC PLANNING

Instructions: Answer the following questions for both "A" and "B":

1. Where are your skills (as listed below) now? (Use an "X")
2. What knowledge levels do you want these groups to have? (Circle the #)

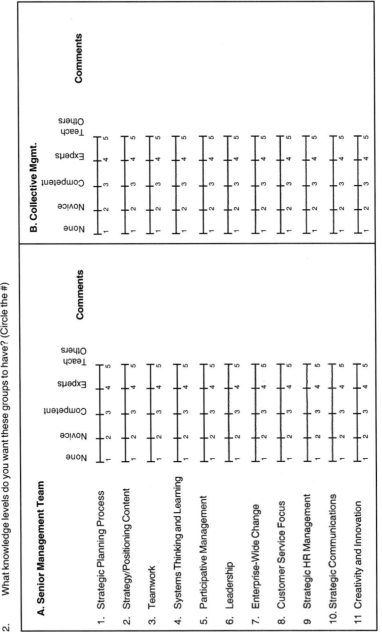

A. Senior Management Team

Scale: None (1), Novice (2), Competent (3), Experts (4), Teach Others (5) — Comments

1. Strategic Planning Process
2. Strategy/Positioning Content
3. Teamwork
4. Systems Thinking and Learning
5. Participative Management
6. Leadership
7. Enterprise-Wide Change
8. Customer Service Focus
9. Strategic HR Management
10. Strategic Communications
11. Creativity and Innovation

B. Collective Mgmt.

Scale: None (1), Novice (2), Competent (3), Experts (4), Teach Others (5) — Comments

3. Discuss and decide: What development do we want to have during the Strategic Planning Process? Right after the planning? Later?

EBRSP-1.pmd

1420 Monitor Road • San Diego • California • 92110-1545 • (619) 275-6528 • Fax (619) 275-0324

PART B
DETAILS OF THE TEN-STEP
STRATEGIC MANAGEMENT SYSTEM

GOAL #1: STRATEGIC PLANNING
Develop a Strategic Plan and Document
(Steps #2-7)

Plans are Nothing.

Planning is Everything.

—Dwight D. Eisenhower

Beware of the SPOTS Syndrome

(Strategic **P**lan **O**n **T**op **S**helf...Gathering Dust)

—Steve Haines

STEP #2

CREATE YOUR OWN FUTURE

If you do not think about the future,
you cannot have one.
—John Galsworthy

"The future belongs to
those who believe in their dreams."

—Eleanor Roosevelt

"The only limits,
as always, are those of vision."

—James Broughton

"You can and should shape
your own future; because, if you
don't, somebody else surely will!"

—J. Barker

We need to learn how to spend
our time and effort working on the future,
instead of continually rearranging the past.

—Philip Crosby

1420 Monitor Road • San Diego • California • 92110-1545 • (619) 275-6528 • Fax (619) 275-0324

IDEAL FUTURE STEP DEFINITION

1. **Vision: Aspirational — Idealistic** *"Our Guiding Star"*
   - Our view/image of what the ideal future looks like at time "X"
   - It has dreamlike qualities, future hopes and *aspirations,* even if they are never fully attainable
   - An energizing, positive, and inspiring statement of *where and what we want to be* in the future

2. **Mission: Pragmatic — Realistic** *"Our Unique Purpose"*
   - What business are we in? (not the activities we do)
   - **"Why we exist** — our reason for being" (raison d' être)
   - The purpose towards which we commit our work life
   - **What we produce**; its' benefits/outcomes
   - **Who we serve** — our customers/clients

3. **Core Values: Our Beliefs** *"What We Believe In"*
   - How do we/should we act while accomplishing this business/mission?
   - "The way we do our business" — *our process*
   - Principles that guide our daily behaviors
   - What we believe in and how we will act at work

4. **Positioning: Our Driving Force — Distinctiveness** *"Our Competitive Edge"*
   - Grand strategy–strategy–strategic intent–competitive advantage
   - What positions us uniquely in the marketplace that causes the customer to do business with us — **Customer Value**

5. **Rallying Cry: Our Essence — Motivational Force** *"Our Memorizable Essence"*
   - The crisp slogan (8 words or less) that is remembered by the employees and is *the essence* of the vision, mission, and core values (i.e., our driving force/positioning upon which all else revolves)
   - It should be a powerful motivational force for our staff as it is memorable, memorized, believable, repeatable and **lived on a daily basis across the organization** — everywhere and in every way

EBRSP-2.pmd

1420 Monitor Road • San Diego • California • 92110-1545 • (619) 275-6528 • Fax (619) 275-0324

VISIONING

Visioning is a process that enables us to put aside reason *temporarily* and look beyond the present to the future as we would like it to be.

"It can't be done" is irrelevant. How to turn a vision into a reality is something that happens after the vision is created.

A Vision Must Be:

1. Leader initiated
2. Shared and supported
3. Comprehensive and detailed
4. Positive and inspiring:
   - a reach
   - a challenge

"Create the Vision Community"

"Vision in Action Can Change the World"

SOME VISION BOUNDARIES

	Step #1: List Current Boundaries.
• Specifics at a future year, decade, etc. • Our markets, customers • Our values, culture • Our core competencies and capabilities • Our driving forces, distinctive characteristics • Our geographic arena • Our history, environment, competitors, industry • Our governance (public, private, shareholders, not-for-profit, etc.) • It is the ideal we want • Answers the "why" we exist; do what we do; societal needs (i.e., good/service to others) • Our level of leadership, excellence, service, quality, etc. • What we are known for; our reputation, image • SKEPTIC — external environmental scan • SWOT • Business Excellence Architecture™ modules • Key Stakeholder list	

EBRSP-2.pmd

1420 Monitor Road • San Diego • California • 92110-1545 • (619) 275-6528 • Fax (619) 275-0324

GOAL SETTING

Goal setting and careful goal selection (i.e., establishing a vision or purpose and meaning) is the #1 criteria for success in all the literature.

> "The best way to predict
>
> your future is
>
> to create it."
>
> —Steve Covey, *"7 Habits"*

FUTURE VISIONING PROCESS

List ideas and brainstorms of the ideal future vision.

Ideal Future Vision at Year _____

MISSION DEVELOPMENT TRIANGLE EXERCISE

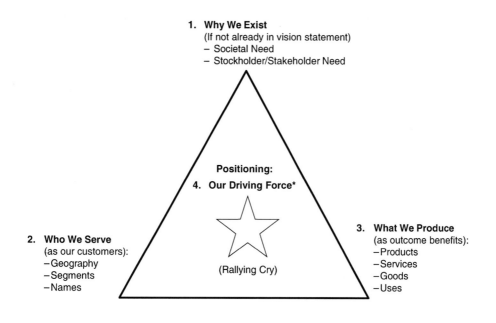

1. Why We Exist
(If not already in vision statement)
– Societal Need
– Stockholder/Stakeholder Need

Positioning:
4. Our Driving Force*

(Rallying Cry)

2. Who We Serve
(as our customers):
–Geography
–Segments
–Names

3. What We Produce
(as outcome benefits):
–Products
–Services
–Goods
–Uses

—Not in Your Mission—
5. What Primary Activities/Tasks We Do

6. How We Operate
– Values, Beliefs, Philosophies
– Major Activities, Techniques, Support Services
– Technologies, Methods of Sale/Distribution,
Capacity
– SBUs and Core Strategies
– Core Competencies and Capabilities

*Note: Your Driving Force can be either a who, a what, a why, or a how (1-2-3-5-6), but it must position you in the marketplace differently from your competitors.

Adapted from: P. Below, G. Morrisey, B. Acomb, *"Executive Guide to Strategic Planning,"* 1978.
S. Haines, *"Internal Sun Co., Inc. Working Paper,"* 1979; updated 1996
J.W. Pfeiffer, L.D. Goodstein, and T.M. Nolan, *"Applied Strategic Planning: A How To Do It Guide,"* Pfeiffer & Co., San Diego, CA 1986.

EBRSP-2.pmd

COMPETITIVE POSITIONING STATEMENT

Also called: Positioning – Driving Force – Grand Strategy – Competitive Edge – Competitive Advantage – Strategic Intent – Image – Brand Reputation – Identity – Value Proposition – Value-Added – Provider of Choice

- Defines our Driving Force(s) as **"the way we differentiate ourselves"** vs. the competition. Sometimes called "the mother of all Core Strategies" as it defines "how we are driven" as an organization.

- It is the main way we achieve a sustained competitive advantage/edge vs. the competition over time .

- Our Rallying Cry is derived from and reinforces this position.

- We must be a "monomaniac with a mission" over time to make this our distinctive competency and reputation.

- *Note:* Customer-focused/oriented organizations do this via 1 of the 5 points on the World-Class Star (★) Results Model of customer wants/needs.

- Be sure you are **not** noncompetitive (i.e., are "ballpark competitive") in all other key areas of customer wants and needs.

EBRSP-2.pmd

1420 Monitor Road • San Diego • California • 92110-1545 • (619) 275-6528 • Fax (619) 275-0324

POSITIONING DEFINED – EXERCISE

Positioning:

What is . . .

- Unique, different, and better about us (world-class),
- Than all the competition in our marketplace (relatively)
- In the "eyes" of the customer, client, or member (perception)
- That motivates the customer to do business with us (growth)

What is their Positioning?

(Q-S-R-C-T or nothing)

1. Marriott Corporation
2. Toyota Motor Corporation
3. Levi Strauss
4. Ritz Carlton
5. Southwest Airlines
6. Singapore Airlines
7. Wal-Mart
8. DHL (Shipping Company)
9. Nordstrom's Department Stores
10. Sony Corporation
11. General Motors
12. General Electric
13. IBM
14. Harley-Davidson
15. Dell Computer
16. McDonalds

EBRSP-2.pmd

1420 Monitor Road • San Diego • California • 92110-1545 • (619) 275-6528 • Fax (619) 275-0324

CREATING CUSTOMER VALUE: POSITIONING

Perceived Customer Value = $\dfrac{\text{Outputs}}{\text{Inputs}}$ = Multiple Outcomes

Question: What does this Star mean to you? Define it in your words.

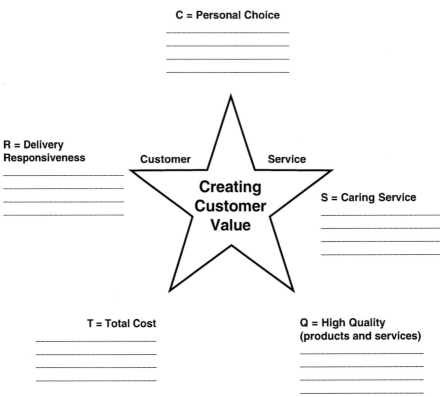

C = Personal Choice

_____

_____

_____

_____

**R = Delivery
Responsiveness**

Customer   Service

**Creating
Customer
Value**

S = Caring Service

T = Total Cost

**Q = High Quality
(products and services)**

*Anticipating Customers' Wants and Needs
For Products, Services and the Intangibles*

Through the Systems Thinking Approach™

EBRSP-2.pmd

1420 Monitor Road • San Diego • California • 92110-1545 • (619) 275-6528 • Fax (619) 275-0324

FINALIZING YOUR DRIVING FORCE EXERCISE

COMPETITIVE POSITIONING STATEMENT

Step 1

From all your core strategies, which is the most important and is actually your driving force? (i.e., What do you believe should be the future driving force(s) for our organization?)

Maximum 1–2; See "Driving Force Defined."

1.

2.

Note: If you have more than two, rethink your list based on the driving force definition.

Step 2

Discuss/come to agreement on this as a consensus with the Core Planning Team and key stakeholders (very important).

Step 3

Now define and write your Competitive Positioning Statement.

RALLYING CRY DEFINED

I. It is:

1. The essence of the vision and mission (i.e., our "driving force" . . . either the who, what, or why).

2. 6–8 words or less.

3. Not an advertising slogan, but for long-term internal use (over the length of the Strategic Plan).

4. Used for internal emphasis/motivation of staff to the vision; it should be a powerful motivational force.

5. A phrase that is memorable, memorized, believable, and able to be repeated on a daily basis across the organization—everywhere and in every way.

6. Often used externally (especially in the not-for-profit sector), but this is secondary.

II. It should be the very last thing developed during strategic planning, once the entire plan is completed and clear.

III. Implementation is often through:

— a contest?

— with rewards (bronze, silver, gold)?

— focused on the criteria for a rallying cry (#1 above)

Note: Keep in mind that the rallying cry is the essence of your vision/mission and thus any decision on it must be made by those most knowledgeable about it (i.e., CEO/ senior executive/core planning team) . . . and not an employee committee, a PR department, or an advertising firm.

1420 Monitor Road • San Diego • California • 92110-1545 • (619) 275-6528 • Fax (619) 275-0324

CRITERIA FOR A CORE VALUE

If we want it to be a core value at year _____, then at that time we want it to meet the following five criteria:

1. It is a collective belief organization-wide . . . simple, clear, and understandable.

2. It determines the "norms" or standards of acceptable behavior as to "how to approach" your work.

3. People know and care when the value isn't being followed.

4. It is an enduring value and consistent over time. It is one of the last things you would want to give up.

5. There are myths, rituals, and other stories to support its existence and it is driven and crystalized from the top.

> There can't be very many like this.
> Core values are few in number.

Adapted from: S.Haines, *"Internal Sun Co., Inc. Working Paper,"* 1979.
J.W. Pfeiffer, L. D. Goodstein, and T. M. Nolan, *"Applied Strategic Planning: A How toDo It Guide,"* Pfeiffer & Co., San Diego, CA, 1986.

EBRSP-2.pmd

1420 Monitor Road • San Diego • California • 92110-1545 • (619) 275-6528 • Fax (619) 275-0324

PERSONAL VALUES EXERCISE

Please rank order these from 1 to 15 with 1 being the most important to you personally and 15 being the least important to you personally.

		Actual	Desired
1.	Having good relationships with colleagues	☐	☐
2.	Professional reputation/respect	☐	☐
3.	Achievement of organization/unit goals	☐	☐
4.	Teamwork and collaboration	☐	☐
5.	Leisure time for enjoyment/fun	☐	☐
6.	Wealth and prosperity	☐	☐
7.	Fitness and health	☐	☐
8.	Contribution/service to society/community	☐	☐
9.	Acknowledging/recognizing other's achievements	☐	☐
10.	Autonomy/freedom to act	☐	☐
11.	Personal growth	☐	☐
12.	Time with family/close friends	☐	☐
13.	Ethical behaviors	☐	☐
14.	Excitement and challenge	☐	☐
15.	Spiritual/religious time	☐	☐

Adapted from: S. Haines, *"Internal Sun Co., Inc. Working Paper,"* 1979.
J.W. Pfeiffer, L.D. Goodstein, T.M. Nolan, *"Applied Strategic Planning: A How to Do It Guide,"* Pfeiffer & Co., San Diego, CA, 1986.
T. Rusk, *"Ethical Persuasion Working Paper,"* 1989, and continued client feedback ever since.

EBRSP-2.pmd

ORGANIZATIONAL VALUES EXERCISE
("Guides to Behavior")

Complete Column #2 (The Way It Should Be): Select 10 of the following values that have the most importance to your organization's future success.

Complete Column #1 (The Way It Is Now) at a later time (or as directed).

Column #1 The Way It is Now (Can Also be Ideal)	Column #2 The Way You Think it Should Be Ideally		
_____	_____	1.	Flexibility/Adaptability to Change
_____	_____	2.	Long Term Strategic Thinking/Perspective
_____	_____	3.	Energizing/Visionary Leadership
_____	_____	4.	Risk Taking/Courage/Integrity
_____	_____	5.	Innovation/Creativity
_____	_____	6.	Marketplace Aggressiveness/Focused
_____	_____	7.	Teamwork/Collaboration
_____	_____	8.	Individual/Team/Organization Learning
_____	_____	9.	Recognition of Achievements
_____	_____	10.	Waste Elimination/Cost Conscious
_____	_____	11.	Accountability/Responsibility
_____	_____	12.	Quality Products/Services
_____	_____	13.	Customer Service Excellence
_____	_____	14.	Speed/Responsiveness
_____	_____	15.	Continuous/Process Improvement
_____	_____	16.	Growth Oriented
_____	_____	17.	Contribution to Society/Community
_____	_____	18.	Safety
_____	_____	19.	Stability/Security
_____	_____	20.	Ethical and Legal Behavior
_____	_____	21.	High Staff Productivity/Performance
_____	_____	22.	Employee Development/Growth
_____	_____	23.	Dialogue/Openness and Trust/Feedback
_____	_____	24.	Constructive Confrontation/Problem Solving
_____	_____	25.	Respect/Caring for Individuals/Relationships
_____	_____	26.	Quality of Work Life/Morale/Satisfaction
_____	_____	27.	Employee Self-Initiative/Empowerment
_____	_____	28.	Participative Decision-Making/Involvement
_____	_____	29.	Data-Based Decisions
_____	_____	30.	Diversity and Equality of Opportunity

Adapted from: S. Haines, *"Internal Sun Co., Inc. Working Paper,"* 1979; J.W. Pfeiffer, L.D. Goodstein, T.M. Nolan, *"Applied Strategic Planning: A How to Do It Guide,"* Pfeiffer & Co., San Diego, CA, 1986; T. Rusk, *"Ethical Persuasion Working Paper,"* 1989; and client feedback ever since.

EBRSP-2.pmd

1420 Monitor Road • San Diego • California • 92110-1545 • (619) 275-6528 • Fax (619) 275-0324

GUIDING PRINCIPLES FOR ENTERPRISE-WIDE CHANGE™

These Core Values are the ones that seem to work best as Guiding Principles for a successful Enterprise-Wide Change process.

- Learning and Knowledge Transfer

- Creativity and Innovation

- Courage and Integrity

- Teamwork and Participation/Involvement

- Speed and Responsiveness

- Holistic and Systemic Orientation

- Flexibility and Adaptablilty

- Openness and Feedback

- Accountability and Responsibility

- Customer and Service-Oriented

- Relationships, Commitments, Sharing and Connectedness

EBRSP-2.pmd

ATTUNEMENT OF PEOPLE'S HEARTS AND MINDS

CORE VALUES ASSESSMENT AND USES THROUGHOUT ALL FOUR PHASES OF A HIGH PERFORMING ORGANIZATION

The following are typical categories where Core Values should appear and be reinforced within an organization. Where else should they appear and be reinforced in your organization?

A 1. **Strategic Plan**

- Explicit corporate philosophy/values statement—visuals on walls; in rooms

B 2. **Feedback**

- This analysis
- Employee Survey
- 360º Feedback

C 3. **Links to Strategies**

- Annual Department Plan Actions
- Performance evaluation; appraisal forms (assess values adherence); team rewards

Alignment of Delivery Processes

D₁ 4. **Operational Tasks/Processes**

- Corporate and product advertising
- New customers and suppliers vs. current customer and supplier treatment and focus (vs. values)
- Operational processes resulting in quality and service

5. **Structure**

- Dealing with difficult times/issues (i.e., layoffs, reorganizations)
- Organization and job design questions

6. **Resources/Technology/Communications**

- Internal communication (vehicles/publications)
- Press releases, external publications/brochures
- Image nationwide (as seen by others)
- Resource allocation decisions

Attunement of People's Hearts and Minds

D₂ 7. **Leadership**

- Flow of orientation and assimilation versus sign-up
- Job aids/descriptions
- New executive start-up
- To whom and how promotions occur (values consequence assessed); criteria
- Executive leadership ("walk the talk"); ethical decisions; how we manage

8. **HR Processes and Practices**

- Recruiting handbook; selection criteria
- How applicants are treated (vs. values)
- How "rewards for performance" operates (vs. values), especially non-financial rewards
- Role of training; training programs (vs. values)
- Policies and procedures (HR, finance, administrative, etc.); day-to-day decisions

9. **Teams**

- Cross-departmental events, flows, tasks forces/teams

Enterprise-Wide Change Management Process

D₃ 10. **Macro**

- Managing change (according to values)
- Stakeholder relationships (vs. values)

EBRSP-2.pmd

ORGANIZATIONAL CULTURE DEFINED

THE WAY WE DO BUSINESS AROUND HERE

Organizational culture is a set of interrelated beliefs or norms shared by most of the employees of an organization about how one should behave at work and what activities are more important than others.

Assumptions/Philosophy =
Our World View
("Weltanschauung")

∨

Personal Values

∨

Organizational Values

∨

Norms of Behavior
(i.e., the standards for action)

∨

Individual Behavior

∨

**Collectively
Leads to Our
Culture**

STEP #3

KEY SUCCESS MEASURES DEFINED

Key success measures are the **quantifiable outcome measurements of success** in achieving an organization's vision, mission, and values on a year-by-year basis to ensure continual improvement towards achieving the ideal future vision.

i.e.,:

1. How do you know if you're being successful?

2. How do you know if you're going to get into trouble?

3. Now, if you are off course (in trouble), what corrective actions do you need to take to get the organization back on track to achieve your ideal future vison?

> The key is to measure:
> **what's important**
> *not*
> **what's easy!**

KEY SUCCESS MEASURES ARE SPECIFIC AND QUANTIFIABLE

i.e.,

1. **Quality**
    - as perceived by customer (surveys?)
    - internal (zero defects)

2. **Quantity**
    - numbers (#)
    - ratios
    - specific existence/non-existence of "x"

3. **Time**
    - 1998-year/Jan-month
    - 3 times a year

4. **Cost**
    - dollars ($)
    - percents (%)
    - ratios

EBRSP-3.pmd

1420 Monitor Road • San Diego • California • 92110-1545 • (619) 275-6528 • Fax (619) 275-0324

KSM SCREENING CRITERIA

REGARDING A KSM

1. It is a "key one" organization-wide (10 or less).

2. It is preferably an output (vs. a means to an end).

3. It has three parts:

    (1) area

    (2) indicator

    (3) measurable targets (baseline, intermediate, and target goal for end of the planning horizon)

4. It has no overlapping or duplicate KSMs among them.

5. It is specific and measurable/quantifiable.

6. It is a key indicator of organization success; it is **not** a comprehensive list— the "comprehensive list" is better served at each department or division (and is even questionable there).

7. It is one you can physically see the status of, so you know factually whether or not it has been achieved.

8. It is a report card (not activities/work plan).

9. It is one you are willing to be a **"monomaniac with a mission"** to achieve year after year.

1420 Monitor Road • San Diego • California • 92110-1545 • (619) 275-6528 • Fax (619) 275-0324

THE QUADRUPLE BOTTOM LINE™ – BALANCE

The Systems Thinking Approach™ to Key Success Measures (KSMs)

1. Employees
   a. Operations

2. Customers

3. Stockholders (Owners)

4. Stakeholders (Community/Society)

Note: The popular "Balanced Scorecard" concept is not a systems approach, but it covers some of the same KSM areas that we do, especially 1, 2, and 3.

Holistic View—Key Success Measures

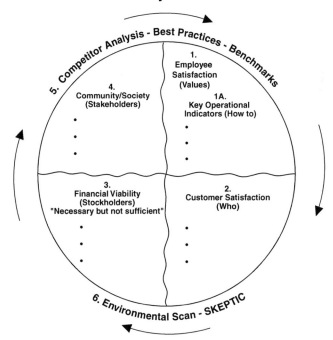

1420 Monitor Road • San Diego • California • 92110-1545 • (619) 275-6528 • Fax (619) 275-0324

KSM AREAS DETERMINED

Individually:

1. What are the key words and phrases from our vision, mission, core values, and driving force(s) statements (that define "success")?
   List them here.

2. What are other key important financial/operational success areas?
   List them here.

3. Combine your answers to the above with the rest of the planning team members into a consolidated list. Then prune it to 10 or less KSM areas.

KSM CONTINUOUS IMPROVEMENT MATRIX (BACKWARDS THINKING)

PRIVATE SAMPLE

KSM Overall Coordinator for is ___Bob Brown, MIS Manager___ (Name/Title)

KSM Areas (Headers) with Specific Factors for Each	Baseline Target 2003	Intermediate Targets 2004	2005	2006	Target 2007	Ultimate Target	Specific KSM Coordinator	KSM Achievement Accountability
1. Employee Satisfaction Factor: Conduct a yearly survey (vs. our Core Values) with a valid sample of our employees (use 10 point scale)	— Develop survey — Conduct it — Revise future targets	6.0/10	7.0/10	8.0/10	8.5/10	10/10	SH	
2. Customer Satisfaction Factors: A. Conduct a quarterly survey of a valid sample of our customers	— Determine their wants for quality products/ services (Focus Group) — Develop/conduct survey — Revise future targets — Benchmark vs. top 3 — Conduct assessment vs. 7 Tracks	7.5/10	8.0/10	9.0/10	9.5/10	10/10	CH	
B. Develop a "close to the customer" culture	— Develop full program with milestones set		Full re-assessment/ refine plan		Full re-assessment/ refine plan	Culture achieved		
		— To be determined during baseline (1999) —						
C. Set up a successful "Mystery Shopper Program"	— Use customer wants to set up program with evaluation scale; milestones					10/10	DM	
		— To be determined once program set (1999)—						
3. Financial Viability Factors: A. ROE B. % Profit (NIAT) C. EPS D. Revenue Growth per Year	— Measures all factors — Revise future targets	TBD 10%/year TBD 15%/year						

Note: These baseline targets must go on Priority Actions List for first year's Annual Planning.

EBRSP-3.pmd

1420 Monitor Road • San Diego • California • 92110-1545 • (619) 275-6528 • Fax (619) 275-0324

KSM CONTINUOUS IMPROVEMENT MATRIX
(BACKWARDS THINKING)

PUBLIC SAMPLE

KSM Overall Coordinator for is ___Mary Smith, Controller___ _____ (Name/Title)

KSM Areas (Headers) with Specific Factors for Each	Baseline Target 2005	Intermediate Targets 2006	2007	2008	Target 2009	Ultimate Target	Specific KSM Coordinator	KSM Achievement Accountability
1. Teamwork/Partnerships Factors:								
A. # of partnerships in existance	— 0	5 9/10	8	10	13	All key areas 10/10	SH	
B. Yearly evaluation of their effective-ness vs. their charter (10 pt. scale)	— Develop Eval. System & Charter Format						DM	
2. Strategic Plan Effectively Implemented (i.e., Strategic Management System) Factors:								
A. SCLSC meets regularly	— 1 day/quarter							
B. Yearly comprehensive map developed and followed each year	— yes — 100%							
C. All management evaluated in new appraisal form (using strategies and values as tools)—HR Audits	— develop appraisal; train mgmt.	100% eval.						
D. Vital Few projects completed successfully	— develop plan to phase in all 4 with targets — leadership program	Organization Restructuring Completed	Quality/ Service Completed	BPR Completed	New Game Plan Devel-oped (all 4)	100% of all targets met		
E. Yearly SMS Review conducted —Action Plan developed —SP & Annual Plan updated	completed — N/A	yes	yes	yes	yes			
3. Self-Funding Factor:								
A. Percent of budget self-funding	— Develop game plan — Begin implementation with time tables	20%	40%	60%	90%	100%	CH	
4. Decentralized Site Based Management Concept Function-ing Effectively	— Develop concept and terminology/evaluation tool — Train mgmt. on it — Benchmark it vs. top 3 competitors	Yearly independent assessment 33% effective	50% effective	75% effective	95% effective	100% effective	JM	

Note: These baseline targets must go on Priority Actions List for first year's Annual Planning.

1420 Monitor Road • San Diego • California • 92110-1545 • (619) 275-6528 • Fax (619) 275-0324

KSM COORDINATOR

1. Keep KSM Matrix up-to-date.

2. Coordinate the collection and reporting of KSM status.

3. Report on actual vs. target — every 2–3 months — to the Strategic Change Leadership Steering Committee (SCLSC).

4. Coordinate with others to develop specific KSMs that are not in existance today.

5. Coordinate baseline data development actions and then baseline data collection.

6. Other duties as assigned:

   — Fully responsible for some specific KSM data collection and reporting
   — Communications of plan/KSM to organization
   — Coordinate Strategic Change Leadership Steering Committee agenda and logistics.

SKILLS/QUALIFICATIONS

1. Highly respected

2. Access to senior management

3. Good with numbers and economics

4. Good computer skills

5. Good lateral skills and relationships

Who is your KSM Coordinator? _____

1420 Monitor Road • San Diego • California • 92110-1545 • (619) 275-6528 • Fax (619) 275-0324

CASCADING KSMs & MEASURING PERFORMANCE

Business Performance Managment System

Organizations that effectively *manage performance* through an integrated and aligned Business Performance Management System achieve superior business results.

> *A "Business Performance Management System"*
> *uses scorecards and good measures as a foundation for*
> *effective deployment and alignment of plans.*

Annual Deployment Cycle
(Performance Scorecard Management Cycle™)

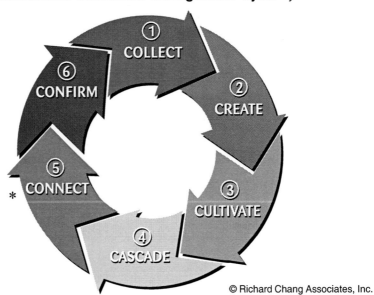

© Richard Chang Associates, Inc.

* Phase 5 - "Connect" is where you link to our *"High Performance Management Cycle"*

EBRSP-3.pmd

1420 Monitor Road • San Diego • California • 92110-1545 • (619) 275-6528 • Fax (619) 275-0324

SCORECARD LINKAGE: "LINE OF SIGHT"

Vertical and Horizontal Linkages

*Scorecards are not isolated; they are linked vertically and horizontally
to other scorecards in the organization*

* Workgroup denotes a business unit, major function, department, or team.

The Cascade-Vertical Linkages

EBRSP-3.pmd

1420 Monitor Road • San Diego • California • 92110-1545 • (619) 275-6528 • Fax (619) 275-0324

LINE OF SIGHT: CONNECT YOUR SCORECARD

(To Your Individual "High-Performance Management System")

In the Connect phase, you continue the cascade process to individual employees, connecting scorecard measures with individual performance scorecards and results. You then provide on-going coaching support, and eventually, hold employees accountable through their performance evaluations.

Phase 5: CONNECT

1. **Individual Performance Plans (for focus)**
2. **Individual Scorecards (for feedback and continuous improvement)**

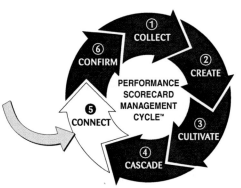

"Connect" to the High-Performance Management Cycle
The Performance Management Cycle Consists of Three Phases:
Planning, Coaching, and Evaluating

1420 Monitor Road • San Diego • California • 92110-1545 • (619) 275-6528 • Fax (619) 275-0324

STEP #4

CURRENT STATE ASSESSMENT

(TEN MINIMUM CURRENT STATE ASSESSMENT AREAS)

Instructions: When conducting your Current State Assessment, it is important to conduct a minimum number of analyses and scanning. The following are those recommended minimums. Please complete this task to ensure that these assessments are conducted as part of your strategic planning.

What To Do	Who To Prepare It Or Do It	By When (Or At What S.P. Mtg/Step)
1. SWOT Analysis		
2. Organizational Culture Survey/Core Values Audit		
3. Positioning vs. competition in the eyes of the customer (Positioning Quotient Survey)		
4. SBU/MPA Information — Pro Forma Matrix Today — Product/product line (market share and profitability)		
5. Organization financial analysis: — P/L (or budgets) — Balance sheet		
6. Yearly Strategic Management Cycle and Audit		
7. Six People Edge Best Practice Areas		
8. "Focus on the Vital Few": a. Market-Oriented Data b. Customer-Focused Organization Assessment c. Strategic Business Design (Building on Baldrige Assessment) d. Strategic Leadership Development System (Leadership Assessment)		
9. Rewards for Total Performance		
10. All Key Success Measures (baseline data on KSM Matrix)		

1420 Monitor Road • San Diego • California • 92110-1545 • (619) 275-6528 • Fax (619) 275-0324

SWOT FRAMEWORK

I. Internal to the Organization/Department (In Here)

Strengths — "Build On"	**W**eaknesses — "Eliminate/Cope"

II. External to the Organization/Department (in the Environment–Out There)

Opportunities— "Exploit"	**T**hreats — "Ease/Lower"

EBRSP-4.pmd

1420 Monitor Road • San Diego • California • 92110-1545 • (619) 275-6528 • Fax (619) 275-0324

—STRATEGIC MANAGEMENT ASSESSMENT—
THREE CORPORATE-WIDE CORE COMPETENCIES

Required of Every Successful Organization in the World

Keyword	Meaning	How to coordinate/ensure it succeeds
#1 DEVELOP LEADERSHIP	Core Competency #1 *"DEVELOP & ACHIEVE LEADERSHIP EXCELLENCE"* Leadership Development System	Employee/Executive Development Board (plus Yearly Leadership Assessment)
#2 PLANNING CYCLE	Core Competency #2 *"BUILD AN INTEGRATED STRATEGIC MANAGEMENT CYCLE"* Overall Strategic Management System	Plannning/Strategic Change Steering Comittee (plus Annual Strategic Review)
#3 INTEGRATED CHANGE	Core Competency #3 *"CREATE A STRATEGIC BUSINESS DESIGN WITH WATERTIGHT INTEGRITY – TO YOUR VISION"* Integrated architecture of structures, processes, people, and systems to achieve Business Excellence	Strategy Sponsorship Teams, Innovation and Change Project Teams (plus *Building on Baldrige* Yearly Best Practices Assessment)

"Leading Enterprise-Wide Change™"
Means
Leading the Development, Installation and Maintenance
of All Three Corporate-Wide Core Competencies
to Achieve Business Excellence.

EBRSP-4.pmd

1420 Monitor Road • San Diego • California • 92110-1545 • (619) 275-6528 • Fax (619) 275-0324

TRIANGLE OF STRATEGIC COMPETITIVE BUSINESS ADVANTAGES

Customer Orientation
(52%)

The Rebuilding of America

Product Quality
(28%)

Innovation
(11%)

The Rest
(9%)

Question: What do you think the percentages are today?

Source: B. Gale (speaker), June 8, 1987, *Linking Shareholder Value to Competitive Advantage,* (PIMS Data Base)

EBRSP-4.pmd

1420 Monitor Road • San Diego • California • 92110-1545 • (619) 275-6528 • Fax (619) 275-0324

CURRENT ASSESSMENT OF CUSTOMER VALUE
"Star ★ Results"
Assessment of What The Customer Values

Score 1 (Low) to 10 (High) or H-M-L

Customer Values Alts: 1. Competition 2. Customer Segments	We Deliver	#1 Choice/Control	#2 Service/ Relationships	#3 Quality Products/ Services	#4 Delivery/Speed/ Convenience (Repsonsiveness)	#5 Total Cost	Point Totals/ Overall Comments
1.							
2.							
3.							
4.							
5.							
6.							
7.							
8.							

EBRSP-4.pmd

1420 Monitor Road • San Diego • California • 92110-1545 • (619) 275-6528 • Fax (619) 275-0324

> ## Beginning of Corporate-Wide Core Competency #3
> ## Integrated Change – to Watertight Integrity

STRATEGIC BUSINESS DESIGN (SBD)

Using Our "Business Excellence Architecture" Model

Best Practices Organizational Assessment

> It is no longer centralized vs. decentralized
> but
> strategic consistency **and** operational flexibility

- **Question:** How do you design your business, leadership, organization, processes, and people practices to support your Ideal Future Positioning and Core Strategies?

- **Answer:** With an integrated and holistic Strategic Business Design for your entire organization, maximizing its synergy to achieve your vision (i.e., **watertight integrity** of design)

See the Centre's **"Business Excellence Architecture"** model for a holistic and integrated Systems Thinking Approach.

Some Topics of a Strategic Business Design:

1.	Shared visions/values	and	shared strategies
2.	Shared values	and	strong culture
3.	Strategies	and	tactics
4.	Formal structure	and	formal design
5.	Strategic consistency	and	operational flexibility
6.	Centralization	and	decentralization
7.	Job descriptions	and	roles/responsibilities
8.	Policies and procedures	and	accountability
9.	Functions	and	business processes
10.	Compensation	and	rewards/recognition
11.	Full-time employees	and	part-time/contract employees
12.	Positioning/core competencies	and	outsourcing/strategic alliances
13.	Product-based	and	customer-focused

> **Mission → Strategy → Structure →"Strategic Business Design"**

ENTERPRISE-WIDE ASSESSMENT

Best Practices Assessment

This Organization-Wide Assessment is designed to evaluate, in a specific and comprehensive way, the present features of your organization. With that knowledge, and a Future Vision, your organization is set on a course for Enterprise-Wide Change™, leading to business excellence.

A Best Practices Assessment Instrument

The Centre for Strategic Management, in partnership with Carla Carter & Associates, has researched and built this comprehensive and insightful "Best Practices Assessment" that incorporates the seven basic components of a Business Excellence Architecture.

This is based on the Malcolm Baldrige National Quality Award Criteria for Performance Excellence, and the combined Best Practices Research of the Centre for Strategic Management, Carla Carter & Associates, and the National Institute of Standards and Technology. This valuable tool is designed to *evaluate* an organization's Current State and *focus in* on specific critical modules/components of the organization that need to change to create Customer Value.

"Business Excellence Architecture™"

is a model mentioned throughout this book. It is a visual graphic of this Enterprise-Wide Assessment Instrument

CENTRE FOR STRATEGIC MANAGEMENT®
Architects of Strategic Change
www.csmintl.com

Carla Carter & Associates, Inc.
www.ChangeExcellence.com

EBRSP-4.pmd

1420 Monitor Road • San Diego • California • 92110-1545 • (619) 275-6528 • Fax (619) 275-0324

COMPETITIVENESS TRIANGLE

We suggest considering the assessments below on your own and, depending on your Strategic Direction, performing some of them. Further details of some of these assessment can be found in the pages following.

External Assessments (OT)	Internal Assessments (SW)
I. **Customers/Marketplace** • Customer-Focused • Customer Recovery Strategy • Marketplace Data/Research II. **Products/Services** • Products/Services • Customer Service III. **Competition** • Competitor Analysis • Search for Substitutes	1. Financial Analysis • P/2 (or Budgets) • Balance Sheet 2. All Key Success Measures 3. Leadership Skills & Competencies 4. Quality & Process Improvement 5. Core Values/Cultural Audit 6. People-Edge Best Practices 7. Employee Needs 8. Rewards/Incentives/Recognition System

I. Customers/Marketplace

Positioning

II. Products/Services   III. Competitors/Substitutes

EBRSP-4.pmd

1420 Monitor Road • San Diego • California • 92110-1545 • (619) 275-6528 • Fax (619) 275-0324

KEY COMMANDMENTS OF CUSTOMER-FOCUSED ORGANIZATIONS

Customer-Focused Organizations

1. Are "close to the customer"—especially senior executives (i.e., see, touch, feel, meet and dialogue with them face-to-face on a regular basis out in the marketplace).

2. Executives—include the customers in their decisions, focus groups, meetings, planning and deliberations.

3. Know and anticipate the customers' needs, wants and desire—continually, as they change.

4. Surpassing customer needs is the driving force of the entire organization.

5. Survey the customers' satisfaction with our products and services on a regular basis

6. Have a clear "positioning" in the marketplace vs. the competition in the eyes of the customer.

7. Focus on Creating Customer Value—i.e., "value-added" benefits to the customer through our Star ★ Results Model (**Quality** products and services, **Customer Choice**, **Responsiveness**, delivery, speed, **Service** vs. **Total Cost** of doing business with you).

8. Set quality customer-service standards—expectations that are specific and measurable to **each department**.

9. Customer Service Standards are based on customer input and focus groups.

10. Require everyone in the organization to experience **moments of truth** by meeting and serving the customer directly...at least one **day every year.**

11. Focus and reengineer the business processes based on the customer needs and perceptions...and do it across all functions.

12. Focus the organization structure based on the marketplace—i.e., structure the organization by customer markets (1 customer = 1 representative).

13. Reward customer-focused behaviors (especially cross-functional teams that work together to serve the customer).

14. Have a clear policy...and the heavy use of recovery strategies to surpass customer expectations.

15. Hire and promote "customer friendly" people.

1420 Monitor Road • San Diego • California • 92110-1545 • (619) 275-6528 • Fax (619) 275-0324

"CUSTOMER RECOVERY STRATEGY" (CRS) DESIGN CHARACTERISTICS

FOR UNSURPASSED CUSTOMER SERVICE

At the "Moment of Truth":

1. Focus on the 5-10 year ROI of the customer.

2. Focus on your long-term image and reputation. (Remember, unhappy people tell 11 others; happy customers tell 4 others.)

3. Empower the person at the "moment of truth" to be creative and innovative to surpass the customer's expectations as to solving the *problem*.

4. Provide expenditure authority to do the above.

5. Ensure accountability = responsibility—at the "moment of truth."

6. Focus recovery on future business (i.e., 50% next time; free next time, etc.).

7. Speed up the recovery—at the "moment of truth."

8. Develop a "Customer Guarantee" and live up to it/surpass it.

9. Ensure your CRS deals with fast responsiveness, being knowledgeable, having empathy and sensitivity, as well as both the tangibles and intangibles.

10. What else?

Five Levels of Recovery Strategy Mastery: Which do we do?

_____ 1. Deny it's our problem. (I just work here.)

_____ 2. Fight their concern but eventually give in to them. (They won.)

_____ 3. Meet their expectations. (Customer is always right.)

_____ 4. Meet their expectations and then do something else beyond it that they don't expect (including an apology).

_____ 5. Do #4 and fix the underlying system or process problem of which it might be a symptom.

EBRSP-4.pmd

1420 Monitor Road • San Diego • California • 92110-1545 • (619) 275-6528 • Fax (619) 275-0324

MARKETPLACE WORKSHEET

Strategic Business Unit/Date _____

Instructions: Define A through G below for either ☐ Today or ☐ Desired in the next three years for our:

A. Main Market Segments	B. Key Customers	C. Main Products and Services	D. Value of Market Segment (H-M-L)	E. Market Share	F. Main Industry Competitors	G. Industry's Life Cycle

EBRSP-4.pmd

1420 Monitor Road • San Diego • California • 92110-1545 • (619) 275-6528 • Fax (619) 275-0324

PRODUCT/MARKET CERTAINTY MATRIX
("Z MODEL")

Products (or Product Lines)

	Existing	New, but Related	New and Unrelated
Existing	90% *Very High Certainty*	60%	30%
New, but Related	60%	40%	20%
New and Unrelated	30%	20%	10% *Very Low Certainty*

Markets (Customer Segments)

Adapted from Hayden and A.T. Kearney (1987 FIMA tape)

1. New products/same customers = 60% success rate.
2. New products/new customers = serious problems with any success.

EBRSP-4.pmd

Best Practices Report
International Quality Study

American Quality Foundation (AQF)
and Ernst & Young

Summary of Study

- extensive statistical study
- 945 management practices over 580 organizations (84% response rate)
- in U.S., Japan, Canada, Germany
- automotive, banking, computer, health care industries

Best Practices Lead to High Performance (defined as:)

1. Market performance (perceived quality index)
2. Operations (productivity) performance (value-added per employee)
3. Financial performance (ROA)

Only Three Universally Beneficial Practices

- Three universally beneficial practices have a significant impact on performance, regardless of starting position (other factors are a question of "fit" to the organization, its environment, and current level of performance):

    1. Strategic Planning/Deployment (Implementation) - A "Strategic Management System/Yearly Cycle"

    2. Business Process improvement methods (if focused on the customer) - Integrated Efficiencies

    3. **Continuously increasing the breadth and depth of leadership and management practices (to make additional gains in performance)**

Background

- Fundamental organizational activities — managing people, processes, technology, and strategy

Leadership is the #1 Organization-Wide Core Competency of all organizations!

EBRSP-4.pmd

1420 Monitor Road • San Diego • California • 92110-1545 • (619) 275-6528 • Fax (619) 275-0324

"SEVEN NATURAL RINGS OF REALITY"

(Taken from "7 Levels of Living Systems")

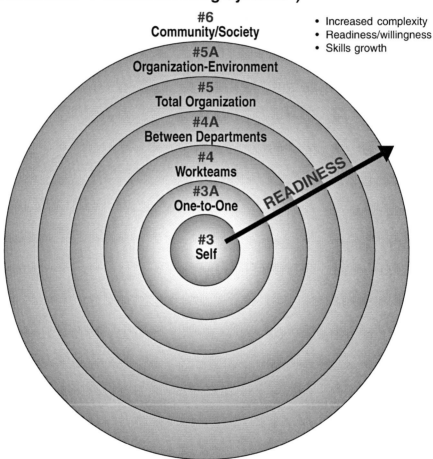

- Increased complexity
- Readiness/willingness
- Skills growth

#6
Community/Society

#5A
Organization-Environment

#5
Total Organization

#4A
Between Departments

#4
Workteams

#3A
One-to-One

#3
Self

READINESS

Note: Rings 3–4–5–6 are 4 of the "7 Levels of Living Systems"
Rings 3A–4A–5A are "Collisions of Systems" interacting with other systems

Source: Stephen G. Haines, 1980; updated 1988, 1994, and 2003

EBRSP-4.pmd

1420 Monitor Road • San Diego • California • 92110-1545 • (619) 275-6528 • Fax (619) 275-0324

THE CENTRE'S LEADERSHIP DEVELOPMENT COMPETENCIES

BEST PRACTICES RESEARCH

Centering Your Leadership	27 Other Authors
1. Enhancing Self-Mastery	1. 27 out of 27 had a similar item
2. Building Interpersonal Relationships	2. 17 out of 27 had a similar item
3. Facilitating Empowered Teams	3. 6 out of 27 had a similar item
4. Collaborating Across Functions	4. 3 out of 27 had a similar item
5. Integrating Organizational Outcomes	5. 13 out of 27 had a similar item
6. Creating Strategic Alliances	6. 9 out of 27 had a similar item

Note: None had all 6 competencies.

- Only 3 had four competencies
- Only 4 had three competencies

CSM does not do basic research. We do action research as well as summarize and synthesize the research of others.

We are translators and interpreters of Best Practices Research.

Management as a Profession

Managers generally don't devote the time and energy to skills that are essential for effective leadership management and communication.

What are they?

Why is it a profession?

How do you make this transition?

EBRSP-4.pmd

1420 Monitor Road • San Diego • California • 92110-1545 • (619) 275-6528 • Fax (619) 275-0324

LEADERSHIP COMPETENCIES—360° FEEDBACK

"Six Natural Levels of Leadership Competencies—found nowhere else"

For Use as: (1) An Organizational Analysis
(2) A 360° Assessment by Self—Supervisor—Others

For Either: (1) Ideal Job Importance and/or (2) Current Job Performance

Six Competencies, 30 Skills, and six key Motivators/Energizers for 21st Century

I. Enhancing Self Mastery: 1. Personal Goal Setting 2. Balancing Body-Mind-Spirit 3. Acting with Conscious Intent 4. Ethics and Character Development 5. Accurate Self-Awareness	**IV. Collaborating Across Functions** 16. Installing Cross-Functional Teamwork 17. Integrating Business Processes 18. Institutionalizing Systems Thinking 19. Valuing and Serving Others 20. Managing People Processes
II. Building Interpersonal Relationships: 6. Caring 7. Effectively Communicating 8. Mentoring and Coaching 9. Managing Conflict 10. Creativity and Innovation	**V. Integrating Organizational Outcomes** 21. Organizing Effectively 22. Mastering Strategic Communications 23. Cascade of Planning 24. Leading Cultural Change 25. Organizing and Designing
III. Facilitating Empowered Teams: 11. Practicing Participative Management 12. Facilitating Groups 13. Delegating and Empowering 14. Training Others 15. Building Effective Teams	**VI. Creating Strategic Positioning** 26. Scanning the Global Environment 27. Reinventing Strategic Planning 28. Networking and Managing Alliances 29. Positioning in the Marketplace 30. International Effectiveness

Energizing and Motivating Forces:

31. Level #1: Has Desire to grow and develop
32. Level #2: Has Reputation for Integrity
33. Level #3: Recognizes Interdependence with others
34. Level #4: Values Providing Service to Others
35. Level #5: Agrees with the Organization's Vision and Values
36. Level #6: Believes in mutual influence/synergistic efforts

EBRSP-4.pmd

1420 Monitor Road • San Diego • California • 92110-1545 • (619) 275-6528 • Fax (619) 275-0324

DEMING'S 14 STEPS TO QUALITY

AN ASSESSMENT

Our Current
State? (H-M-L)

_____   1.   Drive out fear

_____   2.   Eliminate quotas and numerical goals.

_____   3.   Break down all barriers between departments.

_____   4.   Eliminate inspection. Learn to build products right the first time.

_____   5.   Institute a vigorous program of education and self-improvement.

_____   6.   Remove barriers that rob workers of their right to pride of workmanship.

_____   7.   Institute leadership: The aim of leadership should be to help people do a better job.

_____   8.   Eliminate slogans, exhortations, and production targets.

_____   9.   Adopt a new philosophy. This is a new economic age. Western managers must awaken to the challenge, learn their responsibilities, and take on leadership for change.

_____   10.   End the practice of awarding business based on the price tag. Move toward a single supplier for any one item. Base this long-term relationship on loyalty and trust.

_____   11.   Improve constantly and forever the system of production and service.

_____   12.   Put everybody to work to accomplish the transformation.

_____   13.   Institute job training.

_____   14.   Create constancy of purpose toward improvement of product and service to become competitive and to stay in business and to provide jobs.

Adapted from **USA Today**, 11/15/90

1420 Monitor Road • San Diego • California • 92110-1545 • (619) 275-6528 • Fax (619) 275-0324

TYPICAL PROCESSES TO REENGINEER

VALUE ADDING AND CREATING COLLECTION OF ACTIVITIES (ALL BASED ON CUSTOMER NEEDS/WANTS)

I. External Customer

1. Customer-focused product development — customers wants/needs to target/ design to prototype; includes focus groups, surveys, market research, analysis, segmentation, brainstorming, design purchasing, engineering, prototype manufacturing.

2. Customer acquisition — target to proposal to order/sale; includes marketing, segmentation, research, advertising, promotion, prospecting sales, closing.

3. Order fulfillment/manufacturing — order to payment/distribution; includes credit, order entry, assembly, setup, suppliers, procurement, packaging, shipping.

4. Customer service — receipt/inquiry to resolution; includes receipt of product/ service ("moment of truth"), complaints, repairs, customer treatment, speed and response time, etc.

5. Product life-cycle ending — from product use ending with disposition; including reduce reuse, recycle, reclaim, dispose, etc.

II. Other Customers (Stockholders/Owners/Government/Management)

6. Financial management — credits/debits to profit/loss; includes taxes, governments, cash management inventory, investments, profit/loss, balance sheet, capital requirements.

7. People management — recruiting to terminating; includes recruiting, hiring, orienting, developing, rewarding, motivating, promoting, retaining, terminating.

8. Public and investor relations — reality to image/reputation; incudes PR, contributions, communications, reports, relationships, stockholders, media, community.

1420 Monitor Road • San Diego • California • 92110-1545 • (619) 275-6528 • Fax (619) 275-0324

SIX PEOPLE EDGE BEST PRACTICE AREAS

Best Practices Research: Over 30 authors research (see HR bibliography)

Centre for Strategic Management	Key HR Authors
1. Acquiring the Desired Workforce	1. 6 out of 8 had a similar item
2. Engaging the Workforce	2. 8 out of 8 had a similar item
3. Organizing High Performance Teams	3. 1 out of 8 had a similar item
4. Creating a Learning Organization	4. 5 out of 8 had a similar item
5. Facilitating Cultural Change	5. 5 out of 8 had a similar item
6. Collaborating With Stakeholders	6. 5 out of 8 had a similar item

Note:
- None had all 6 competencies.
- Only 2 out of 8 even had any of the beginning elements of a systems oriented approach to strategic human resource management and planning

The Centre does not do basic research. We do **action research** as well as summarize and synthesize the research of others. We are **translators and interpreters**.

Developed by Allan Bandt, Stephen Haines, and James McKinlay, Centre for Strategic Management.

1420 Monitor Road • San Diego • California • 92110-1545 • (619) 275-6528 • Fax (619) 275-0324

BEST PEOPLE PRACTICES

The Systems Thinking Approach to Creating the People Edge

I. The Six Levels of People Edge Best Practices

Area 1: Acquiring the Desired Workforce (The Individual) 1. Individual capability requirements 2. Alternative workforce arrangements 3. Workforce, succession, and retention planning 4. Career development 5. Recruiting methods to hire the desired employees	**Area 4: Creating a Learning Organization (Interdepartmental)** 16. Spreading learning and intellectual capital 17. Institutionalizing Systems Thinking 18. Measuring Human Resources 19. Valuing debriefing events/projects/processes 20. Encouraging creative thinking
Area 2: Engaging the Workforce (Interpersonal) 6. Performance management systems 7. Compensation systems 8. Recognition systems 9. Flexible benefit programs 10. Dealing with poor performance	**Area 5: Facilitating Cultural Change (Organization)** 21. Desired organization culture 22. Developing the collective management skills 23. Aligning and streamlining all Human Resource processes 24. Organizing change structures 25. Developing strategic change experts
Area 3: Organizing High Performance Teams (Team) 11. Developing teams 12. Developing small unit team leaders 13. Empowering work teams 14. Participative management skills 15. Rewarding and reinforcing teamwork	**Area 6: Collaborating with Stakeholders (Organization–Environment)** 26. Operating in a global environment 27. Maintaining strategic alliances 28. Positive people environment 29. Focusing on customers 30. Balancing value contribution

II. More Inputs: Leadership Roles and Six Leadership Development Competencies 31. Defining roles in creating The People Edge 33. Developing Leadership Competencies. 34. Partnering with management 35. Adding Human Resource value 36. Articulating the strategic direction	**III. The Fundamental Core Input: Strategic Human Resource Planning** 37. Developing a Strategic Human Resource Plan **IV. The Outer Circle: Outcomes and Results** 38. Alignment with the Corporate Strategic Plan 39. Attunement of People's Hearts and Minds 40. Number One Core Competency—our strategic leadership competency

Developed by Allan Bandt, Stephen Haines, and James McKinlay, Centre for Strategic Management.

EBRSP-4.pmd

1420 Monitor Road • San Diego • California • 92110-1545 • (619) 275-6528 • Fax (619) 275-0324

EMPLOYEE NEEDS QUESTIONNAIRE

WHAT DO EMPLOYEES WANT FROM A PERFORMANCE MANAGEMENT SYSTEM?

List in priority rank order (1-10) your needs from your current job.

Priority		Need
Survey Results	Yours	
		1. Higher salary and/or more benefits
		2. Recognition for doing good work
		3. Food, clothing, and shelter
		4. Satisfying the boss' wishes
		5. Promotion to a better job
		6. Personal growth and development
		7. Safety in your work environment
		8. Prestige and status
		9. Job security
		10. Opportunity for independent thought and actions (freedom)

EBRSP-4.pmd

1420 Monitor Road • San Diego • California • 92110-1545 • (619) 275-6528 • Fax (619) 275-0324

NATIONWIDE SURVEYS (TIME-AFTER-TIME)

TOP THREE JOB "NEEDS" OF EMPLOYEES

1. Recognition for doing good work
2. Freedom for independent thought and action
3. Opportunity for personal growth

OTHER "NEEDS"

4. Higher salary and/or more benefits.
5. Promotion to a better job.
6. Job security.
7. Satisfying the boss's wishes.
8. Prestige and status.

Sources: Dr. H. Migliore, Dean, Oral Roberts Business School, and hundreds of other similar surveys across North America and Europe by Stephen G. Haines.

EFFECTIVE REWARDS ARE ...

- Timely
- Significant
- Personally meaningful
- Competing against oneself only
- Multiple winners

Note: "Pay for Performance" violates all of these. Hence, the need for a different type of "reward"—a "non-financial" reward.

EBRSP-4.pmd

1420 Monitor Road • San Diego • California • 92110-1545 • (619) 275-6528 • Fax (619) 275-0324

INTERNAL ASSESSMENT — PERFORMANCE & REWARDS

REWARDS FOR TOTAL PERFORMANCE ASSESSMENT

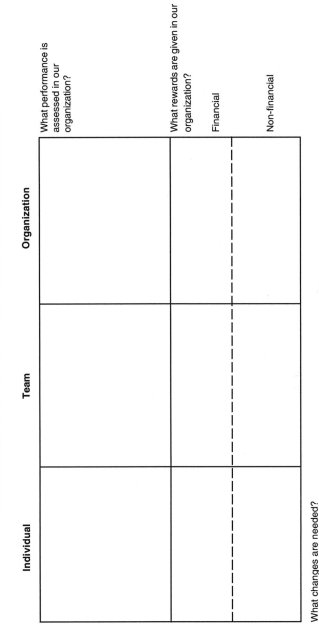

	Individual	Team	Organization
What performance is assessed in our organization?			
What rewards are given in our organization?			
Financial			
Non-financial			

What changes are needed?

Who is responsible to lead this change?

EBRSP-4.pmd

1420 Monitor Road • San Diego • California • 92110-1545 • (619) 275-6528 • Fax (619) 275-0324

AN OLYMPIC RECOGNITION PROGRAM THAT WORKS

(REWARD AT 3 LEVELS — BRONZE — SILVER — GOLD)

Some Key Concepts

1. Select 1-2 key outcomes you want, based on your Strategic Plan, such as lower costs, improved customer service, etc. Reward results and achievement, not ideas or suggestions.

2. The key program nomination characteristics include:
    - Anyone can nominate anyone else or any team, including themselves.
    - Nominations are for anyone or any team that has actually achieved an outcome desired above.

3. Ideas and proposals are **not** rewarded; achieving actual results are rewarded (i.e. save $11.00, receiving a customer service thank you, etc.)

4. Publicize this program widely. Set up a simple one-page form on colored paper to fill out. Make the form widely distributed and available.

5. Hold large group meetings on a regular basis (quarterly?) with everyone eligible in attendance. If the organization is spread out, hold regional meetings and possibly one big annual meeting. It is best to make this meeting a quarterly business meeting with the *recognition* of winners as the main attraction. Some other business topics might include:
    - Discussion of Key Success Measures or business outcome results.
    - A guest speaker on a key topic, such as one of your key strategies or core values.
    - Discussion of 1-2 key core strategies and their importance and priorities.
    - Celebration of successes—social time such as a buffet lunch, end of day non-alcoholic happy hour, etc.

6. Set up a Peer Review Committee to review submissions for documented outcomes. The goal is to cultivate as many "winners" as possible – not to create a contest of winners and losers. You compete against yourself, not others. Keep results secret until the meeting.

7. A basic analogy is the **"Olympic Games"** bronze, silver and gold winners. For example Bronze might be for those who "win" during a particular quarter; Silver might be the top ten semi-annual winners; and Gold would be awarded to the top 3-5 "'best and brightest" of the year. Do not single out one big final winner!

1420 Monitor Road • San Diego • California • 92110-1545 • (619) 275-6528 • Fax (619) 275-0324

STEP #5

STRATEGY AND PRIORITIES DEFINED

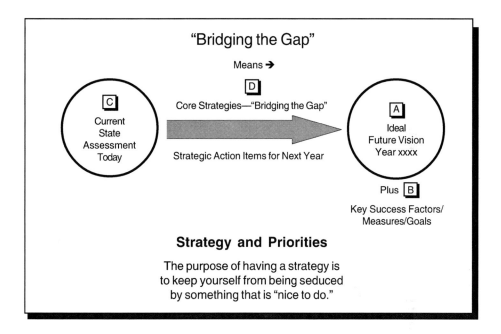

"Bridging the Gap"

Means →

D

Core Strategies—"Bridging the Gap"

Strategic Action Items for Next Year

C
Current State Assessment Today

A
Ideal Future Vision Year xxxx

Plus B

Key Success Factors/ Measures/Goals

Strategy and Priorities

The purpose of having a strategy is to keep yourself from being seduced by something that is "nice to do."

What is a Strategy?

- It is **the criteria** or **basic approaches** we use to guide individual and organizational behaviors toward the achievement of our organization's vision.

- It is also seen as the **major or key ways, methods**, and **groups of activities** we use to guide us in "bridging the gap" over the life of the strategic plan—from your Current State Assessment to your Ideal Future Vision.

- It **defines the "how-to's" or major ways** we will use to reach the attainment of our vision and mission.

- Strategies should also be few in number; generally 2-7 (maximum). Fewer strategies better allow a focused direction by the organization.

- **Strategies are the primary _"means"_ to the _"ends"_ (Ideal Future Vision).**

EBRSP-5.pmd

1420 Monitor Road • San Diego • California • 92110-1545 • (619) 275-6528 • Fax (619) 275-0324

CORE STRATEGIES AND KSMs

(MEANS ➜ ENDS)

Both Important—But Different

Key Success Measures (KSM) are sometimes confused with strategies.
1. Core strategies are the primary "means" to the "end" (Ideal Future Vision).
2. KSMs are usually output or final measurements of this "end" (Ideal Future Vision).

The Guts of Strategic Planning

Strategies and KSMs are the "guts" or "meat" of strategic planning. Thus, they are the two parts of the strategic planning final document that are used by the Strategic Change Steering Committee to track the progress and success of your strategic plan.

In Summary

- KSMs are "outcome measures" of success.
- Core Strategies are the primary "means" to achieving the ends (embodied by the outcome measures).

> *Thus — to some people . . .*
>
> **KSMs = Goals**
>
> *and*
>
> **Core Strategies = Objectives**

1420 Monitor Road • San Diego • California • 92110-1545 • (619) 275-6528 • Fax (619) 275-0324

THE WEB: STRATEGIES AND FUNCTIONS

CORE STRATEGIES ARE LIKE THE WEBBING IN A CHAIR
"The Glue That Holds It All Together"

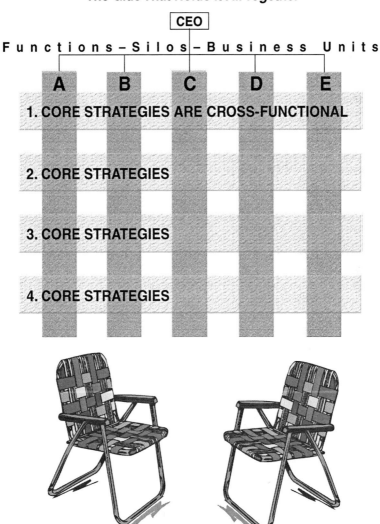

| CEO |

Functions – Silos – Business Units

A   B   C   D   E

1. CORE STRATEGIES ARE CROSS-FUNCTIONAL

2. CORE STRATEGIES

3. CORE STRATEGIES

4. CORE STRATEGIES

EBRSP-5.pmd

1420 Monitor Road • San Diego • California • 92110-1545 • (619) 275-6528 • Fax (619) 275-0324

CRITERIA FOR STRATEGY SELECTION

Strategies are the Major:

- "How To's"
- Methods
- Approaches

(Not an *outcome* or *what*, but a *how to*)

1. Topics needing focus/attention

2. Integrated with each other—not separate at all

3. Support Vision, Mission, and Values Attainment (the "what")—can see how to achieve them

4. Linked to customers/products (Alignment of the delivery products)

5. Linked to people edge (Attunement of people's hearts and minds)

6. Not a comprehensive list—Core Strategies

7. Few in number (less is more)—but clear and specific

1420 Monitor Road • San Diego • California • 92110-1545 • (619) 275-6528 • Fax (619) 275-0324

**"Moving the Strategic Plan and Direction
Down Through the Entire Organization"**

Strategic Consistency
and Operational Flexibility

"You don't implement a Strategic Plan.

You implement the annual tactical or operational plans

built upon the strategic direction."

—Steve Haines

The Cascade of Planning is based on "The 7 Levels of Living Systems".

Question: **What are the two "glues" that bind the organization together down through all of its levels?**

#1: _____

#2: _____

EBRSP-5.pmd

1420 Monitor Road • San Diego • California • 92110-1545 • (619) 275-6528 • Fax (619) 275-0324

PROGRESSIVE STRATEGIES FOR 21st CENTURY

These are some of the primary strategies of the **late 1980s**:
1. High Quality Products (i.e., Ford)
2. Unsurpassed Customer Reputation (i.e., Nordstrom's)
3. Retrenchment, Turn-Arounds, Cost Reductions (i.e., IBM, GM)
4. Divestitures (i.e., Sunoco, LBOs)
5. Growth Through Capital Leverage (i.e., Marriott, Disney)

These are some of the primary strategies of the **1990s**:
1. Flexibility (i.e., Giant Industries)
2. Speed (i.e., Toyota)
3. Horizontally Integrated — Related products/by-products (i.e., Arco's AM/PM Mini-Marts, Ethanol Plants)
4. Networks and Alliances (i.e., Apple/IBM, Japanese Kieretsu's)
5. Value Added — More Value for the Money (i.e., Nissan Maxima "Luxury" Sedan)
6. Environmentally Improved/Based Products (i.e., Solar Heat; Toxic Waste Clean-Up)
7. Commonization/Simplification (i.e., Honda Value Analysis)
8. Business Process Reengineering — BPR (i.e., GE's Workout)
9. Employee Morale/Family Benefits and Part-time Focus on Work (Lots of Firms)
10. Management and Leadership Practices (i.e., GE/Giant)
11. Outsourcing — Cottage Industry (Lots of Firms)
12. Core Competencies — People, Technology, etc. (i.e., Sony)
13. Market Tie-Ins/Preferred Customers (i.e., San Diego Padres/Local Indian Casinos)
14. Cause-Related Marketing (i.e., McDonald's)
15. Data Driven Marketing (i.e., Financial Services)
16. Value Chain Management (i.e., Walmart)

These are some of the primary strategies of the **21st Century**:
1. Lean Electronics (Rockwell)
2. Expanded View of Our Markets (GE)
3. Electronic Commerce (CISCO)
4. "Experiences" (i.e., Planet Hollywood, Adventure Travel)
5. Alternative Delivery Channels (i.e., Internet, Satellite)
6. Organizational Learning (i.e., GE)
7. Mass Customization (i.e., Toyota)
8. Marketing One-to-One (Don Peppers)

EBRSP-5.pmd

1420 Monitor Road • San Diego • California • 92110-1545 • (619) 275-6528 • Fax (619) 275-0324

THE RENAISSANCE IN GOVERNMENT

13 PRINCIPLES OF ENTREPRENEURIAL GOVERNMENT

1. Steer, not row (facilitate vs. do it yourself)

2. Empower communities and customers to solve their own problems rather than simply deliver services.

3. Encourage competition rather than monopolies.

4. Be driven by missions, not rules.

5. Be results-oriented by funding outcomes rather than inputs.

6. Meet the needs of the customer, not the bureaucracy.

7. Concentrate on earning and making money rather than spending it.

8. Stop subsidizing everyone. "User-pay" through charging user fees.

9. Invest in preventing problems rather than curing crises.

10. Decentralize authority.

11. Solve problems by influencing market forces rather than creating public programs.

12. Reduce regulations; cut out bureaucracy and low risk taking.

13. Privatization (except for essentials not provided elsewhere).

Adapted from [1] *Reinventing Government: How the Entrepreneurial Spirit is Transforming the Public Sector* by David Osborne and Ted Gaebler, Addison-Wesley, 1992.; [2] *Governing,* October 1992 (with a rebuttal by H. George Frederickson)

EBRSP-5.pmd

CORE STRATEGIES FINALIZED

As a result of your analysis of the current state/gaps, final ideal future vision, and the "Strategies Profile," answer the following question.

What do you believe are the 3–7 (max) core strategies our organization should pursue over the life of the strategic planning horizon to achieve our ideal future vision.

1.

2.

3.

4.

5.

6.

7.

EBRSP-5.pmd

1420 Monitor Road • San Diego • California • 92110-1545 • (619) 275-6528 • Fax (619) 275-0324

STRATEGIC ACTION ITEMS (SAIs)

For each core strategy, an organization needs a "Plan" or set of major Strategic Action Items over the planning horizon.

These SAIs:

. . . are the major corporate-wide activities, tasks, actions, and changes required *over the planning horizon* to achieve each core strategy—the **must do's!**

Steps

1. Ensure you first have a very clear **strategy statement** for each core strategy to guide the strategic action items.

2. **Add a title** that describes the strategy (three words or less).

3. Ensure you have clarity of any paradigm shifts these entail, i.e. **"From →To" statements** as key phases of the changes.

4. **Brainstorm** 10–15 action items for each strategy over the next three years

5. Limit yourself to **three action priorities** for each strategy to focus the changes that you want to accomplish in **the next 12 months**.

SYSTEMS THINKING:
STRATEGIES LINKED TO MEASURES

Instructions:
1. Fill in your lists of Core Stratetgies and Key Success Measures
2. Take each KSM separately and work horizontally to put a ✓ in each strategy box that helps to achieve the KSM.
3. Once you've completed this task for each KSM, look at the results. **Are you satisfied that doing your Core Strategies will ultimately achieve all your KSMs?**

Key Success Measures ↓ / Core Strategies →	1.	2.	3.	4.	5.	6.	7.	8.	9.
1.									
2.									
3.									
4.									
5.									
6.									
7.									
8.									
9.									
10.									
11.									
12.									
13.									
14.									
15.									

EBRSP-5.pmd

1420 Monitor Road • San Diego • California • 92110-1545 • (619) 275-6528 • Fax (619) 275-0324

"STRATEGIC CHANGE IMPACT EXERCISE"

CREATING A HIGH PERFORMANCE ORGANIZATION
(Using the A–B–C–D–E Phases and the "Organization as a System" Model)

What components of your organization will/should be impacted by the major change/strategy you propose? Which change/strategy?: _____

Which Components are Impacted and How?	Action Needed/Implications
Phase E Environment 1. _____ Environmental Scanning System 2. _____ Key Environmental Stakeholders (List):_____ _____ **Future Environmental Trends/Scan:** 3. _____ S = Socio-demographics 4. _____ K = Competition 5. _____ E = Economics 6. _____ E = Natural Environment 7. _____ P = Political/Regulatory 8. _____ T = Technology 9. _____ I = Industry 10. _____ C = Customers	
Phase A ***Module #8—Creating Customer Value (Quadruple Bottom Line):** 1. _____ Customer Satisfaction 2. _____ Employee Satisfaction 3. _____ Shareholder Satisfaction 4. _____ Community/Society Satisfaction **Customer Positioning Choices:** 5. _____ Quality Services 6. _____ Quality Products 7. _____ Customer Service (Feelings) 8. _____ Customer Choices 9. _____ Lower Cost Products/Services 10. _____ Speed/Responsiveness/ Convenience	

continued

* NOTE: These 8 Modules correspond to the 8 Modules of this Business Excellence Architecture that results in the Building on the Baldrige Assessment Instrument.

EBRSP-5.pmd

1420 Monitor Road • San Diego • California • 92110-1545 • (619) 275-6528 • Fax (619) 275-0324

STRATEGIC CHANGE IMPACT EXERCISE

Which Components are Impacted and How?	Action Needed/Implications?
Module #2—Reinventing Strategic Planning:	
1. _____ Vision	
2. _____ Mission	
3. _____ Organizational Values	
4. _____ Organizational Positioning	
5. _____ Organizational Identity/Image (Brand)	
6. _____ Strategic Business Units	
7. _____ Annual Operating Priorities	
8. _____ Annual Department Plans	
9. _____ Operating Budgets	
10. _____ Capital Budgets	
11. _____ Financing/Banks/Investors	
12. _____ Annual Strategic Review (& Update)	
Phase B	
13. _____ Key Success Measures— Outcome Measures (List): _____ _____ _____	
14. _____ Cascade of metrics to all Management levels	
Phase C	
15. _____ Other Core Strategies (List): _____ _____ _____ _____	

1420 Monitor Road • San Diego • California • 92110-1545 • (619) 275-6528 • Fax (619) 275-0324

STRATEGIC CHANGE IMPACT EXERCISE

Which Components Are Impacted and How?	Action Needed/Implications?
Phase D **Module #1—Building a Culture of Performance Excellence: The Foundation:** 16. _____ Systems Thinking Language/Skills 17. _____ Org'n as a Learning Org'n 18. _____ Innovation & Creativity Language/Skills 19. _____ Adult Learning Theory (Experiential Learning) 20. _____ Group Facilitation 21. _____ Fact-based Decision-making	
Module #3—Leading Strategic Change and Innovation: 22. _____ Organizational Structure 23. _____ Change Management Structures 24. _____ Team Development 25. _____ High Performance Management 26. _____ Strategic Communication Processes 27. _____ Empowerment 28. _____ Key Internal Stakeholders (List): 29. _____ Participative Management & Involvement _____ _____ _____ 30. _____ Change Management Plans/Processes	
Module #4—Creating the People Edge: 31. _____ Strategic People/HR Plans 32. _____ Job Design/Definition 33. _____ Staffing Levels (Recruitment/ Downsizing Selection) 34. _____ Training and Development 35. _____ Performance Appraisal 36. _____ Rewards System (Pay/Non-Pay)	

EBRSP-5.pmd

1420 Monitor Road • San Diego • California • 92110-1545 • (619) 275-6528 • Fax (619) 275-0324

STRATEGIC CHANGE IMPACT EXERCISE

Which Components are Impacted and How?	Action Needed/Implications?
Module #5—Achieving Leadership Excellence:	
37. _____ Succession Planning for Executives & Management	
38. _____ Succession Planning for Key Other Jobs/Roles	
39. _____ Leadership Development System	
40. _____ Job Excellence	
Training & Development:	
41. _____ Executives	
42. _____ Management/Supervisors	
43. _____ Sales & Marketing	
44. _____ Workforce	
Module #6—Becoming Customer Focused:	
45. _____ Strategic Marketing/Sales Planning	
46. _____ Market Research/Customer Needs	
47. _____ Sales Management	
48. _____ Marketing Management	
49. _____ Customer Services	
Module #7: Aligning Delivery:	
50. _____ Daily Operating Tasks	
51. _____ Continuous Process Improvement/Waste Elimination	
52. _____ Business Processes Re-engineered	
53. _____ Simplify Policies & Procedures	
54. _____ Enterprise-Wide Technology	
55. _____ Supply-Chain Management	
56. _____ Facilities & Equipment	
57. _____ Cross-Department Knowledge Transfer	
58. _____ Strategic Business Design	

EBRSP-5.pmd

1420 Monitor Road • San Diego • California • 92110-1545 • (619) 275-6528 • Fax (619) 275-0324

STEP #6

Three-Year Business Planning

For
- **Strategic Business Units (SBUs)**
- **Lines of Business (LOBs)**
  as well as
- **Major Support Departments (Depts)**
- **Major Program Areas (MPAs)**

This is a commonly missed step and a serious omission!

> A Three-Year Business Plan is the most important thing you can do to increase profits, crystallize your thinking and remain afloat.
>
> —*Ed Freiermuth*

1420 Monitor Road • San Diego • California • 92110-1545 • (619) 275-6528 • Fax (619) 275-0324

CASCADE OF PLANNING

I. Strategic Planning Levels

1. Organization-Wide Strategic Planning

You need an organization-wide, 3, 5, or 10-year strategic plan, defining the organization's vision, mission, core values, and key success factors, along with the core strategies for achieving them. (This is organizational Level #5 of the Seven Levels of Living Systems.)

2. Business Unit Strategic Planning (often called 3-Year Business Plans)

You need 3-year business plans for each business unit, major program area, and major support department (such as HR) within the organization. (This is organizational Level #4 of the Seven Levels of Living Systems.)

II. Annual Planning Levels

3. Annual Plans for all Departments/Functional Units (including HR)

Annual operating plans over the next 12 months are needed (and budgets too) for all parts of the entire organization. (This is also organizational Level #4 of the Seven Levels of Living Systems.)

4. Individual Plans, Goals, and Objectives

Individual plans are needed to show how each employee intends to accomplish the goals they must meet in order to carry out the organization-wide strategic plan. You also need to revise your performance appraisals, basing them on core strategies (results) and core values (behaviors). (This is organizational Level #3 of the Seven Levels of Living Systems.)

1420 Monitor Road • San Diego • California • 92110-1545 • (619) 275-6528 • Fax (619) 275-0324

STANDARD BUSINESS PLANNING DOCUMENT

THREE YEAR TIME HORIZON

Outputs for the SBU/MPA/Major Support Departments:

E   Environmental Scanning (SKEPTIC) Ongoing: continued into future

A 1. Ideal Future Vision (or adopt organization-wide vision)

2. Mission Statement/Driving Force(s)

3. Any additional and complimentary Core Values for the SBU/MPA (beyond adotping organization-wide ones?)

4. Definition of target markets and products/services (4 P's):
   — customer segments, demographics
   — competitors, niches, industry, trends
   — product line, areas of service
   — promotion and marketing
   — prices and places of sales (geography)

B 5. Key Success Factors — Financial, Operations, Human Resources
   — SBU or product line, services proforma P/L matrix (on growth over 3 years)

C 6. Current State Assessment:
   — SWOT for SBU/department
   — environmental scanning (SKEPTIC)
   — competitor analysis
   — customers/market analysis
   — product/product line analysis

7. Strategy Development:
   — core strategies
   — strategic action plans for each core strategy over 3 years
   — other major projects over next 3 years
   — specific products, services, expansion
   — specific customers, markets, expansion
   — reduce to concise set of top priority actions for the next 12 months (3 per strategy)

D 8. Next 12 months implementation/change management process

Question: **Are these the Business Planning outputs you want? If not, modify this list.**

EBRSP-6.pmd

1420 Monitor Road • San Diego • California • 92110-1545 • (619) 275-6528 • Fax (619) 275-0324

STRATEGIC CONSISTENCY AND
OPERATIONAL FLEXIBILITY

You don't implement a Strategic Plan

—*but*—

You do implement an Annual Plan*
Based on the Strategic Plan

5-Year Strategic Plan (1)

⬇

3-Year Business/Major Support Dept. Plans (2)

⬇

Annual Plan Priorities and Budgets (3)

⬇

Department Work Plans (4)

⬇

Individual Performance Plans (5)

The Glue: Shared Strategies and Common Values

*Even the Annual Plan must be a **"Living, Breathing Document"**
that is modified, as necessary, throughout the year.

EBRSP-6.pmd

Page 122

STEP #7

ANNUAL PLANS AND BUDGETS

(Two-Page Corporate Yearly "Cheat Sheet" and To Do List)

Instructions: In terms of ensuring our overall success this fiscal year, **what are the top three-four priority action items for each core strategy** which need to be accomplished?

Core Strategies	Who Responsible?	When Done?
Core Strategy #1 1. 2. 3. 4.		
Core Strategy #2 1. 2. 3. 4.		
Core Strategy #3 1. 2. 3. 4.		
Core Strategy #4 1. 2. 3. 4.		
Core Strategy #5 1. 2. 3. 4.		
Core Strategy #6 1. 2. 3. 4.		
Core Strategy #7 1. 2. 3. 4.		

EBRSP-7.pmd

Department: _____

Date: _____
Fiscal Year _____

ANNUAL "WORK PLAN" FORMAT
(AND FOR FUNCTIONAL/DIVISION WORK PLANS ALSO)

#_____ : Strategy/Goals: _____

Yearly Pri #	Action Items (Actions/Objectives/How?)	Support/Resources Needed	Who Responsible?	Who Else to Involve?	When Done?	How to Measure? (Optional)	Status

EBRSP-7.pmd

1420 Monitor Road • San Diego • California • 92110-1545 • (619) 275-6528 • Fax (619) 275-0324

LARGE GROUP ANNUAL DEPARTMENT REVIEWS

(AND LARGE GROUP – WHOLE SYSTEM – TEAM BUILDING)

The Concept:
1. *Small group* presentations by all major department heads (# = _____ Depts.) on their Department Annual Work Plans.
2. *Small group* presentations to the "collective" leadership/management of the entire organization (# = _____ collective management).

Large Ballroom:

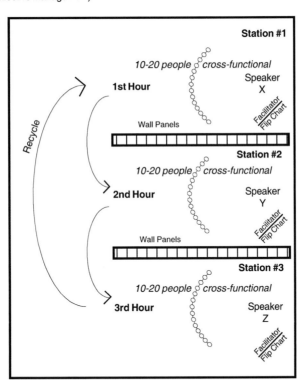

Philosophy: Small group, cross-functional teams meeting together and moving around in hourly activities create greater interaction, more energy, commitment, understanding, buy-in, and teamwork to implement the Strategic Plan.

Large group "dog and pony" presentations are boring at best!

EBRSP-7.pmd

Page 125

TEN WAYS TO ESTABLISH YOUR BUDGET AND RESOURCE ALLOCATION APPROACH

*"If money was what it took to be a success,
then how did Japan and Germany rise from the ashes?"*

Approach #1:   Macro allocations only (let managers decide " how to")

Approach #2:   Activity level budgeting (0-based) conducted

Approach #3:   Require 5-10-15% budget cut projections and plans (cut different amounts though)

Approach #4:   Budget "hold-backs" (create a pool of funds) for strategic priority uses

Approach #5:   Recommend New Initiative Programs (NIPS) for all funding increases

Note: The next five approaches are too late to *begin* at strategic budgeting time. You need to start them earlier in the year, so that their results in cost savings will be evident at budgeting time.

Approach #6:   "Workout" the bureaucracy/eliminate "waste"

Approach #7:   Reengineer your business' economic structure/process

Approach #8:   Learning as a critical resource/increased skills and motivation

Approach #9:   Recognition and rewards programs

Approach #10:   Fund raising

EBRSP-7.pmd

1420 Monitor Road • San Diego • California • 92110-1545 • (619) 275-6528 • Fax (619) 275-0324

SEVEN "MUST DO" PEOPLE PROJECTS/TASKS

(ONCE STRATEGIC PLANNING IS COMPLETE)

1. Redo your **performance appraisal** form/procedures to reward your core strategies and values—i.e. "Line of Sight" cascade from Key Success Measures.

2. Redo your **executive "Performance Management System"** to ensure the Strategic Plan gets down to individual executive accountability . . . and to reinforce and model your core values and strategies.

3. Audit and modify your entire **formal and informal rewards system** (pay and nonpay) to ensure they reinforce and support your future direction.

4. Set up an Executive Development Board to lead the revisions to your **recruiting, hiring, training, succession planning, and promotion** criteria and processes to promote your Strategic Plan and direction with the right people with the right skills in the right jobs to carry out your Vision.

5. Redo your orientation and assimilation processes (i.e., **Smart Start**) to start people off with the right values and culture of your future vision.

6. Redo your **Leadership Development System** to build and reinforce your core values, culture, and future vision — especially leadership and management skills (not just knowledge and awareness) to carry this out successfully.

7. Develop a **Strategic Human Resource Management Department** 3-year "Business Plan" to support the organization-wide Strategic Plan.

1420 Monitor Road • San Diego • California • 92110-1545 • (619) 275-6528 • Fax (619) 275-0324

PERFORMANCE APPRAISALS . . .

TIED TO STRATEGIC PLANNING

Performance Appraisals
must be tied to support

#1
Your organization's Core Strategies (i.e., results)
and

#2
Your organization's Core Values (i.e., behaviors)
and

#3
Your own learning and growth (i.e., career development)
(If you are serious about your Strategic Plan)

— Result: A Four Page Performance Management/Appraisal Form —

❶

Cover Sheet
Summary
Evaluation

❷

Results	
Strategies	Plan/
1.	Actual
2.	
3.	
4.	
5.	

❸

Values	
Values	Plan/Actual
1.	
2.	
3.	
4.	

❹

Career Development	
Objectives	Action Plan
1. __X__ : _____	
2. __Y__ : _____	
3. __Z__ : _____	

EBRSP-7.pmd

1420 Monitor Road • San Diego • California • 92110-1545 • (619) 275-6528 • Fax (619) 275-0324

STEP #8

SMART START™ & PLAN-TO-IMPLEMENT

Major Change Fails 75—80% of the time!

"Successful Implementation"

Two Goals:
- Serve your clients today
- Build for the future (change management—see below)

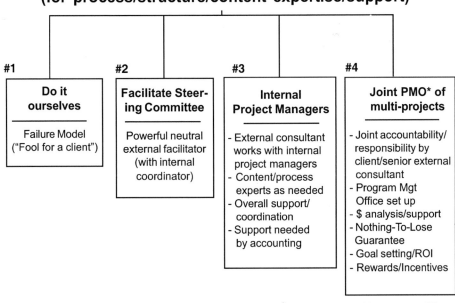

┌─────────────────────────────────────┐
│ **ENTERPRISE-WIDE CHANGE™**   │
│ **Leader is CEO**   │
│ **(Runs Change Leadership Team)**   │
└─────────────────────────────────────┘

**Four Choices on the use of External Consultants
(for process/structure/content expertise/support)**

#1

Do it ourselves
Failure Model ("Fool for a client")

#2

Facilitate Steering Committee
Powerful neutral external facilitator (with internal coordinator)

#3

Internal Project Managers
- External consultant works with internal project managers - Content/process experts as needed - Overall support/ coordination - Support needed by accounting

#4

Joint PMO* of multi-projects
- Joint accountability/ responsibility by client/senior external consultant - Program Mgt Office set up - $ analysis/support - Nothing-To-Lose Guarantee - Goal setting/ROI - Rewards/Incentives

* PMO = Program Management Office

EBRSP-8.pmd

1420 Monitor Road • San Diego • California • 92110-1545 • (619) 275-6528 • Fax (619) 275-0324

"PLAN-TO-IMPLEMENT" DAYS

(EDUCATE—ASSESS—TAILOR—ORGANIZE)

I. **Educate**
1. Iceberg Theory of Change (content – process – structure)
2. Rollercoaster of Change
3. Menu of Structures for Change
4. 3 Goals, 3 Premises, ABCs Model
5. Three Types of Change, Two Ways to Manage It
6. Why Change Fails?

II. **Assess**
1. Summary of Desired Major Changes (from the Strategic Plan)
2. Strategic Plan/Annual Plan completion
3. Year #1 Strategic Change Process
4. Leadership Development Assessment/System
5. Multi-year Cultural Change Effort (Executive Development)
6. "Organizational Systems Design" (Watertight Integrity)

III. **Organize**
1. Change Leadership Steering Committee
2. Strategy Sponsorship Teams (SSTs)
3. Internal/External Coordination (Change Agent Cadre)
4. Employee Development Board
5. Key Success Measure Tracking – measuring
6. Personal Leadership Plans (PLPs)

IV. **Tailor**
1. Yearly Comprehensive Map of Implementation (single page Game Plan)
2. Change Leadership Team (#1 Absolute) – regular meetings – how often
3. Performance/Rewards Form/System to Reinforce the Change
4. Rollout/Communicate to Organization (including Trifold)
5. Strategic People Plan ("Creating the People Edge")
6. Implementing Enterprise-Wide Change (violate the norms)
7. "One Agenda—One Day" meetings on key nuggets

EBRSP-8.pmd

1420 Monitor Road • San Diego • California • 92110-1545 • (619) 275-6528 • Fax (619) 275-0324

MAJOR CHANGE SUMMARY

C A summary of the major changes desired over the entire life of our Strategic Plan.

1.

2.

3.

4.

5.

6.

7.

8.

9.

10.

11.

12.

13.

14.

15.

16.

17.

18.

19.

20.

EBRSP-8.pmd

1420 Monitor Road • San Diego • California • 92110-1545 • (619) 275-6528 • Fax (619) 275-0324

ENTERPRISE-WIDE CHANGE PROCESS™

Why to we need a change process?

It is most difficult for a stable organization to change itself; that is, for the regular structures of the organization to be used for change. They have an investment in the status quo.

Assumptions About the Strategic Change

1. All change is a *loss experience* and stress results.

2. There is a *rational learning curve* that people travel at different dates/speeds.

3. There is an *emotional rollercoaster* that people also uniquely travel when the stress of change is introduced.

4. People have finite amounts of energy. The *real question* is where do they use their time (i.e., "time is a reflection of one's priorities").

5. The loss experience, the *emotional rollercoaster,* and the *learning curve* all take time and energy . . . instead of productive work time.

1420 Monitor Road • San Diego • California • 92110-1545 • (619) 275-6528 • Fax (619) 275-0324

TYPES OF CHANGE MANAGEMENT

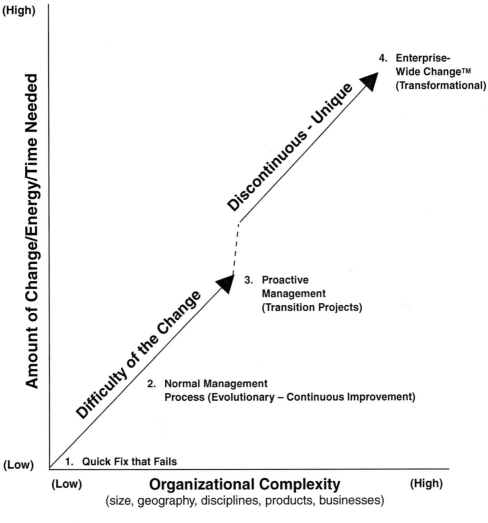

(High)

Amount of Change/Energy/Time Needed

4. Enterprise-
   Wide Change™
   (Transformational)

Discontinuous - Unique

3. Proactive
   Management
   (Transition Projects)

Difficulty of the Change

2. Normal Management
   Process (Evolutionary – Continuous Improvement)

(Low)   1. Quick Fix that Fails

(Low)   **Organizational Complexity**   **(High)**
(size, geography, disciplines, products, businesses)

Types of Change.eps

EBRSP-8.pmd

Page 133

1420 Monitor Road • San Diego • California • 92110-1545 • (619) 275-6528 • Fax (619) 275-0324

ENTERPRISE-WIDE CHANGE™

Characteristics

Yes/No

	1.	Radical and profound or fundamental change is required
	2.	A paradigm change—new rules and boundaries—leap of faith required
	3.	New strategies must be defined
	4.	Desired vision may be clear; however its achievement is tenuous
	5.	Future environment is unclear, uncertain and uncontrollable; could go in multiple directions
	6.	An "emergent journey" will occur as the uncertainty peels away
	7.	Marketplace in turmoil with old stability gone
	8.	Complexity, chaos, and confusion are part of the work-life
	9.	Mobilizing, energetic leadership is required at multiple levels
	10.	Risk of future failure is very high; survival may be an issue
	11.	Cultural and employee change is definitely required
	12.	Some senior management skills may be obsolete; new capabilities needed
	13.	Products, services, customers, and business each may be in question
	14.	Requires death of old company or organization

Totals: Yes_____ ; No _____

Examples

- cultural change
- new businesses
- leap in marketshare
- organization must transform itself
- new operational values

- new company emerging
- new core competencies needed
- new organizational design needed
- some new workforce skills required
- becoming a global company

Visualization

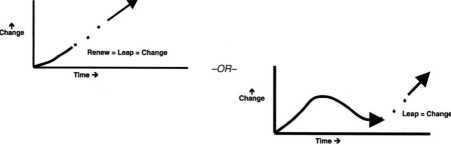

Change ↑

Renew = Leap = Change

Time →

–OR–

Change ↑

Leap = Change

Time →

EBRSP-8.pmd

1420 Monitor Road • San Diego • California • 92110-1545 • (619) 275-6528 • Fax (619) 275-0324

THE ICEBERG THEORY OF CHANGE
The Systems Thinking Approach™

(The CAPACITY* to Achieve Your Competitive Business Advantage)

Efforts:

13%

**1.
CONTENT**
What
(Visible)

"Alignment" – Operational Tasks
(Customer Edge)
• Customer ★ Results
• Delivery Processes

What's Your . . .

. . . Level of Capacity*

87%

COMPETENCIES
RESOURCES

2. PROCESSES – How
(Below the Surface)

"Attunement" – wth People's
Hearts (People Edge)
• Support Content
• Rollercoaster Uses
• Change Processes

3. STRUCTURES – Framework
(Deep Foundation)

"Systems Thinking"
(Strategic Edge)
• Change Structures
• Organizational
Capabilities
• Culture

CULTURE/COMMITMENT

CONTENT MYOPIA

is our failure to focus on Process and Structure.

Yet,

Change is dependent on good *Processes and Structures*

in order to Achieve the *Content* of the desired changes.

MEWC-01

EBRSP-8.pmd

1420 Monitor Road • San Diego • California • 92110-1545 • (619) 275-6528 • Fax (619) 275-0324

ORGANIZATIONAL CAPACITY AND COMMITMENT (CULTURE)

(To undergo Enterprise-Wide Change Successfully)

Instructions: Rate our current Organizational Capacity and Commitment to build and sustain Enterprise-Wide Change on a multi-year basis by the collective leadership and management team as well as all employees.

Scoring: (H—M—L)   Comments:

I. Demonstrated Long-Term Commitment: By the Collective Leadership Team 1. _____ CEO 2. _____ Senior Management 3. _____ Board of Directors 4. _____ Collective Management Team 5. _____ All Employees	1 2 3 4 5
II. Effective change Processes: To facilitate a successful Enterprise-Wide Change process 6. _____ Parallel Involvement Process 7. _____ Rollercoaster of Change Process 8. _____ Wave after Wave of Change Process 9. _____ HR Best People Policies and Practices 10. _____ Strategic Communications Processes	6 7 8 9 10
III. Effective Change Infrastructures: In place to guide the Enterprise-Wide Change process 11. _____ Change Leadership Team 12. _____ Program Management Office/ Change Team 13. _____ Yearly Map of Implementation 14. _____ Innovative Process/ Project Teams 15. _____ Positive Work Culture	11 12 13 14 15
IV. High Level of Capabilities and Competencies: To lead the Enterprise-Wide Change effort effectively 16. _____ Leadership Excellence 17. _____ Business Acumen 18. _____ Daily People Management Practices 19. _____ Systems Thinking Applications (Concepts/Tools) 20. _____ Creativity and Innovation Competencies	16 17 18 19 20
V. Adequate Resources: Devoted exclusively to Enterprise-Wide Change 21. _____ People 22. _____ Time 23. _____ Money 24. _____ Information/Access 25. _____ Equipment/Support/Facilities	21 22 23 24 25

EBRSP-8.pmd

1420 Monitor Road • San Diego • California • 92110-1545 • (619) 275-6528 • Fax (619) 275-0324

ENTERPRISE-WIDE CHANGE™ MANAGEMENT

"A MENU" – STRUCTURES AND ROLES

MAIN STRUCTURES – SENIOR LEADERSHIP

1. **Visionary Leadership** — CEO/Senior Executives with **Personal Leadership Plans (PLPs)**
   - For repetitive stump speeches and reinforcement
   - To ensure fit/integration of all parts & people towards the same vision/values
2. **Internal Support Cadre** — Informal/kitchen cabinet
   - For day-to-day coordination of implementation process
   - To ensure the change structures & processes don't lose out to day-to-day
3. **Executive Committee**
   - For weekly meetings and attention
   - To ensure follow-up on the top 15-25 priority yearly actions from the Strategic Plan
4. **Change Leadership Team** (formal)—replaces or is the Strategic Planning Team
   - For bimonthly/quarterly follow-up meetings to track, adjust and refine everything (including the Vision)
   - To ensure follow-through via a yearly comprehensive map of implementation
5. **Program Management Office** — Joint internal and external experts
   - For Enterprise-Wide Change requiring management of multiple change processes and projects
   - To ensure "Watertight Integrity" to your Vision, Positioning, and Values (Strategic Business Design)

SUB-STRUCTURES – SUBCOMMITTEES

6. **Strategy Sponsorship/Project or ProcessTeams**
   - For each core strategy and/or major change effort / Key Initiatives
   - To ensure achievement of each one; including leadership of what needs to change
7. **Employee Development Board** (Attunement of People's Hearts)
   - For succession – careers – development – core competencies (all levels) – performance management/appraisals
   - To ensure fit with our desired values/culture — and employees as a competitive edge
8. **Technology Steering Committee/Group**
   - For computer — telecommunications — software fit and integration
   - To ensure "system-wide" fit/coordination around information management
9. **Strategic Communications System (and Structures)**
   - For clear two way dialogue and understanding of the Plan/implementation
   - To ensure everyone is heading in the same direction with the same strategies/values
10. **Measurement and Benchmarking Team**
    - For collecting and reporting of Key Success Measures, especially customers, employees, competitors
    - To ensure an outcome/customer-focus at all times
11. **Accountability and Responsibility System**—all levels
    - For clear and focused 3-year business plans and annual department plans that are critiqued, shared and reviewed, as well as individual performance appraisals
    - To ensure a fit, coordination and commitment to the core strategies and annual top priorities
12. **Whole System Participation Team** (can combine with #8)
    - For input and involvement of all key stakeholders before a decision affecting them is made. Includes Parallel Processes, Search Conferences, Annual Management Conferences, etc.
    - To ensure a critical mass in support of the vision and desired changes
13. **Rewards and Recognition Programs** (can combine with #6)
    - For recognizing and paying people for strategic management accomplishments
    - To ensure reinforcement of the Accountability and Responsibilities System
14. **Organization Redesign Team**
    - For studying and recommending what redesign of the organization is needed
    - To ensure synergy of the strategies, structures, processes, policies, values and culture
15. **Environmental Scanning System**
    - For collecting data from the environment (SKEPTIC)
    - To ensure advance awareness of coming changes to the environment

EBRSP-8.pmd

1420 Monitor Road • San Diego • California • 92110-1545 • (619) 275-6528 • Fax (619) 275-0324

ENTERPRISE-WIDE CHANGE™ LEADERSHIP TEAM

Ineffectiveness of Hierarchical "Cascade" Implementation Strategy Alone

The normal "cascade" strategy for implementing change is usually ineffective, because memories remain embedded in the way the organization works after the change. This applies particularly if the change relates to the culture rather than to work practices or systems.

—Dick Beckhard
Changing the Essence

A new way to run your business, giving equal weight to managing desired changes, in addition to the ongoing daily management of the organization.

Purposes

1. To guide and control the implementation of any large scale, enterprise-wide strategic planning/change efforts undertaken through the "Strategic Planning/Clarity of Purpose" or "Seven Business Excellence Architecture Modules for Creating Superior Results."

2. To coordinate any other major performance improvement projects going on in the organization at the same time; to ensure fit with the time and energy demands of ongoing daily business activities (i.e., *systems fit, alignment, and integrity*).

Criteria for Membership

1. Senior management leadership teams for today and the future as well.

2. Informal or formal leaders from parts of the organization that are key to implementation.

3. "Core Steering Group Implementation Staff Support Team", including overall Enterprise-Wide Change management Program Management Office Leaders, KSM/ESS coordinators, and internal facilitators.

4. Credible staff who are knowledgeable of the actual Strategic Plan/Enterprise-Wide Plan that was developed.

5. Key stakeholders who share your ideal future vision and are willing to actively support it.

EBRSP-8.pmd

continued

EXECUTIVE/EMPLOYEE DEVELOPMENT BOARD (EDB) CONCEPT

"Invest in Your People First"

The people management practices of any organization should be viewed as a system of people-flow, from hiring through the length of their careers and retirement and/or termination. See the Centre's copyrighted Strategic People Edge Management model and assessment tools. Making this all happen is the responsibility of senior management; usually best done through an "EDB" (Executive/Employee Development Board) focused solely on this framework and "creating people as a competitive business advantage." *(The "People Edge")*

The EDB reinforces senior management's responsibility for carrying out organization-wide "stewardship" responsibilities. **The best way to carry this out is to create a Strategic "People Edge" Plan that fully defines and implements the corporate Strategic Plan's people strategy.**

In essence, this Executive Stewardship Board is responsible for Human Resource Management flow and continuity. It is their responsibility to link staffing to business strategy via:

- hiring
- selection (up/lateral)
- succession planning/core competencies
- developmental jobs/experiences
- Leadership Development System
- training: classroom (internal, external)

- organization design/structure
- socio-demographic trends
- employee surveys of satisfaction/360º feedback
- rewards/performance system
- workforce planning

A mechanism/structure of how to achieve management continuity is needed (i.e., a linking pin of several Boards):

1. Executive Development Board (EDB)—executive team
2. Management Development Board (MDB)—all department heads/teams
3. Employee Development Committees (EEDC)—all supervisors/section head areas

The desired outcomes include:

Right person — Right job — Right time — Right organization — Right skills!

Sample Monthly Executive Meetings

Week 1	Operational/Business Issues
Week 2	Strategic Planning and Change Process/Status
Week 3	Strategic Change Issues
Week 4	Customer Satisfaction
*Week 5	Executive/Employee Development Board (EDB)
(Quarterly)	Staff, promotion, succession, development – HR Executive as Secretary to Senior Mgt.

EBRSP-8.pmd

1420 Monitor Road • San Diego • California • 92110-1545 • (619) 275-6528 • Fax (619) 275-0324

SUCCESSION PLANNING LEVERAGE

It is "Central" to people as a competitive edge.

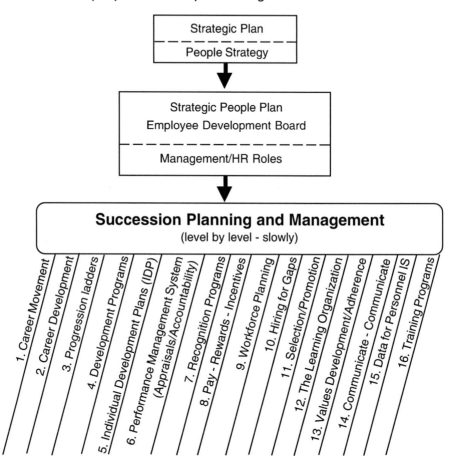

Win - Win:

- Employee Satisfaction
- Positive Work Environment
- Organization Depth for future growth
- Stakeholder returns/satisfaction

1420 Monitor Road • San Diego • California • 92110-1545 • (619) 275-6528 • Fax (619) 275-0324

YEARLY COMPREHENSIVE MAP OF ENTERPRISE-WIDE CHANGE™ IMPLEMENTATION

Year _____   Organization _____

Date(s)	Month	Meeting/Topic	Notes
_____	January		
_____	February		
_____	March		
_____	April		
_____	May		
_____	June		
_____	July		
_____	August		
_____	September		
_____	October		
_____	November		
_____	December		

EBRSP-8.pmd

1420 Monitor Road • San Diego • California • 92110-1545 • (619) 275-6528 • Fax (619) 275-0324

HOW TO MANAGE ENTERPRISE-WIDE CHANGE™

1. Clearly define/agree on the new vision.
2. Set up a "Change Management Steering Committee"

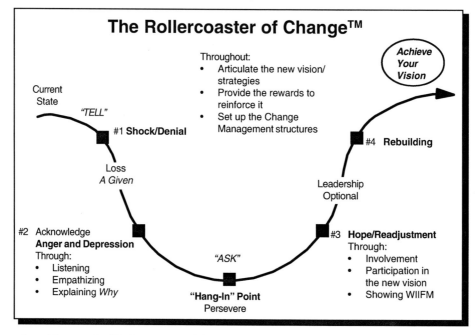

The Rollercoaster of Change™

Current State
"TELL"
#1 **Shock/Denial**

Throughout:
- Articulate the new vision/strategies
- Provide the rewards to reinforce it
- Set up the Change Management structures

Achieve Your Vision

#4 **Rebuilding**

Loss
A Given

Leadership Optional

#2 Acknowledge
Anger and Depression
Through:
- Listening
- Empathizing
- Explaining *Why*

"ASK"

"Hang-In" Point
Persevere

#3 **Hope/Readjustment**
Through:
- Involvement
- Participation in the new vision
- Showing WIIFM

3. Manage the "Rollercoaster of Change™"

Major Questions

1. Not "if" but "when" will we start to go through shock/depression?
2. How deep is the trough?
3. How long will it take?
4. Will we get up the right (optional) side and rebuild?
5. At what level will we rebuild?
6. How many different rollercoasters will we experience in this change?
7. Are there other changes/rollercoasters occurring?
8. Will we "hang-in" and "persevere" at the midpoint (bottom)? How?
9. How will we deal with normal resistance?
10. How will we create a "critical mass" to support and achieve the change?

EBRSP-8.pmd

1420 Monitor Road • San Diego • California • 92110-1545 • (619) 275-6528 • Fax (619) 275-0324

ENTERPRISE-WIDE CHANGE™ AND EXCELLENCE

THE FIVE CHOICES OF CHANGE AND LEVELS OF EXCELLENCE

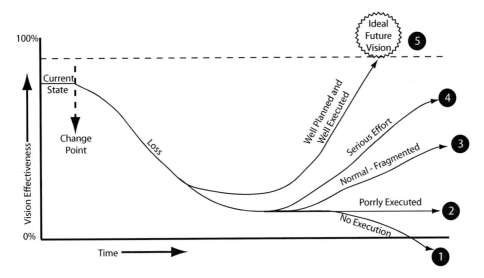

Which will you be?

_____ **1** **Incompetence**—"Going Out of Business"

_____ **2** **Technical** — "Dogged Pursuit of Mediocrity"

_____ **3** **Management** — "Present and Accounted For Only"

_____ **4** **Leadership** — "Making a Serious Effort"

_____ **5** **Visionary Leadership** — "Developing an Art Form"

IDEAS FOR INITIALLY COMMUNICATING THE STRATEGIC PLAN

- Print the plan and distribute it with a cover letter (KISS). Tri-fold on Strategic Plan – One page KSM matrix – One page Annual Plan Priorities – One page Yearly Map of Implementation
- Develop handouts/overhead slides for "standard use" by all executives.
- Hold organization-wide managers meeting to hear directly from the CEO/Executive Director and other members of the planning team. (Also thank them for their help.)
- Hold divisional/department all-employee meetings to ask questions about the plan and pose concerns.
- Hold stakeholder meetings to review results and thank them for their help.
- Hold two-day workshops to learn about strategic planning, to discuss the strategic plan, and to build supporting plans at a unit/site or individual level.
- Require "Strategic Business Planning" process for units/major support functions.
- Develop posters with planning themes.
- Print up individual (plastic) cards with values, mission, and KSMs.
- Make video tapes of the CEO/Executive Director or others explaining the organization's vision and strategies to achieve that vision.
- Publish internal newsletter stories or memos/letters introducing the plan (overall, and then again one piece at a time).
- Publish external news releases and special public feature stories.
- Do *report cards* each quarter — shared with all stakeholders.

Now— how to keep the Plan alive over the next 3-5 years?

LADDER OF COMMUNICATION EFFECTIVENESS

(REPETITION – REPETITION – REPETITION)

One-to-One Conversation

Small Group Discussion

Large Group Discussion

Video Conference

Telephone Conversation

Communication Methods	
Words =	7%
Tone =	38%
Body Language =	55%
Total =	100%

What you do speaks louder than what you say!

Conference Call   "2 way"

Voice Mail   "1 way"

Pager

Handwritten Letter

E-Mail

Fax

Typewritten Letter

Mass-Produced Letter

Newsletter

Brochure

News Item

Advertisement

Handout

We Remember Approximately:

- 10% of what we *read*
- 20% of what we *hear*
- 30% of what we *see*
- 50% of what we *see* and *hear*
- 70% of what we *say* and *do*
- 90% of what we *explain as we do*

Repetition Increases Understanding

- 1st time = 10% retention
- 2nd time = 25% retention
- 3rd time = 40-50% retention
- 4th time = 75% retention

EBRSP-8.pmd

1420 Monitor Road • San Diego • California • 92110-1545 • (619) 275-6528 • Fax (619) 275-0324

STRATEGIC COMMUNICATION GOALS

(FOR SENIOR LEADERS)

("Stump Speeches" Needed)

- Gain greater commitment to the organization's vision, values and strategies.

- Develop more trust and honesty—blunt spoken—speak the unspeakable.

- Build the credibility needed for effective leadership–be human, admit mistakes.

- Focus your organization's efforts on critical issues and top annual priorities.

- Communicate more directly and effectively with a broader constituency—to all stakeholders.

- Identify the organization's key messages over and over again (repetition).

- Use your own personality, passion and voice to greater leverage as a leader—be yourself—be unique

---

Communications and Emotions

Teddy Roosevelt was right about the bully pulpit: "Some look at the evidence and believe that if their conclusions are logical, others should accept them automatically. That's not good enough. You have to communicate—constantly, emotionally, and directly."

—*Time*, November 16, 1992

EBRSP-8.pmd

HOW TO BUILD A CRITICAL MASS

TEN WAYS (THE LILY POND THEORY)

It can take two years to build your critical mass. The following are ways to help you do this:

1. Modify Strategic Plan/Enterprise-Wide Change drafts — listen, review (i.e., the Parallel Process).

2. Continue to hold Parallel Involvement Process meetings with key stakeholders thoughout implementation.

3. Develop trust in your leadership by being open via the Change Leadership Team, Program Management Office and every day — involve skeptics.

4. Developing 3-year Business Plans for all Business Units/Major Support Departments by involving key stakeholders/staff.

5. Develop Annual Plans for all departments/divisions/sections under the Strategic Plan/core strategy umbrella.

6. Put out "updates" after each Change Leadership Team meeting and ask for feedback.

7. Use Innovative Project/Process Teams and/or Strategic Sponsorship Teams as "change agents" and Implementation Vehicles for each core strategy and key initiatives.

8. Implement quick changes/actions so people know you are serious (silent majority).

9. Review reward systems and the performance appraisal form to reinforce core values and core strategies.

10. Answer WIIFM for each person (i.e., political–cultural issues)

Remember that "skeptics are our best friends." If you encounter skeptics during your Parallel Involvement Process, be sure to ask them why they are skeptical. Get them to identify the road-blocks; don't try to force them to agree with you. Those road-blocks are the key items to be sure to overcome to ensure successful achievement of your vision.

Critical Mass Building – It takes almost 2 years to build enough support (i.e., Lily Pads) in an organization (i.e., Lily Pond) to create the critical mass.

Year #1
- Core Strategic Planning/Enterprise-Wide Team
- plus 20-40 key "others"

Year #2
- the rest of the organization
- other key external stakeholders

EBRSP-8.pmd

MULTI-YEAR ENTERPRISE-WIDE CHANGE

Concept: Take the entire Senior Management Collective Leadership Team (up to 30-40 people max) through an intense 2-5 day training and development experience **together 1-2 times per year.**

Then:

Goal: Use it to develop, focus the attention, action plan and kick off of the entire organization's approach to one of a number of key topics of cultural change.

Suggested Sequence/Flow:

I.   Initial Topics (in a tailored order)

I.   Strategic and Systems Thinking

2.   Reinventing Strategic Management

3.   Leading Enterprise-Wide Change

4.   Creativity and Innovation

5.   Strategic Leadership Development

6.   Conflict Management—Ethical Persuasion

7.   Coaching for Commitment

8.   Group Facilitation (and Participative Decision Making) for Leaders

II.   Additional Key Topics in Cultural Change (in no order)

1.   Creating the People Edge

2.   Creating Customer Value

3.   Blowing Out Bureaucracy

4.   Organization and Process Redesign

5.   Learning and the Learning Organization

6.   Effective Team Building (Teams Everywhere)

7.   Negotiating—Win-Win

8.   Train-the-Trainer for Managers

9.   Personal and Supervisory Transition Management

10.   Excellence in Customer Service

1420 Monitor Road • San Diego • California • 92110-1545 • (619) 275-6528 • Fax (619) 275-0324

PERSONAL LEADERSHIP PLAN

To ensure the success of our Strategic Plan, I will need to develop my own personal leadership competencies as well as take specific action to demonstrate my own efforts to anchor my leadership within the organization.

A.   Personal Leadership Development

Competency/Skill	What's to Be Undertaken	Time Frame
1.		
2.		
3.		

B.   Demonstrating Personal Leadership in the next year, I will:

Action	Target Area	By When
1.		
2.		
3.		

Signed: _____   Date: _____

Print Name: _____   Title: _____

EBRSP-8.pmd

Page 149

ENTERPRISE-WIDE CHANGE™ GAME PLAN TEMPLATE

(Based on the Iceberg Theory of Change Framework)

CONTENT OF THE CHANGE:

1. **Enterprise-Wide Change Vision:**
   (Including both economic alignment and cultural attunement issues)

2. **Any Missing Elements from your Clarity of Purpose?**
   (Covered in Chapter Four, regarding E, A and B Phases of the Simplicity of Systems Thinking)

INFRASTRUCTURES FOR THE CHANGE:

3. **Main Enterprise-Wide Change Infrastructures:**
   (Including the Program Management Office, Change Consultants and the Support Cadre plus the Change Leadership Team)

4. **Enterprise-Wide Change Substructures:**
   (Such as an Employee Development Board, Rewards Team, Innovative Process/ Project Teams, Technology Steering Committee, etc.)

5. **Clear Roles for the Players of Change:**
   (All four Roles plus Personal Leadership Plans for all executives, and the Parallel Involvement Process with all employees)

PROCESSES OF CHANGE:

6. **Leading, Managing and Re-creating the Change Processes:**
   (Including the Rollercoaster of Change's Six Stages, the Waves and waves of change, and the HR/People processes to support them)

ENTERPRISE-WIDE CHANGE COMPETENCIES, COMMITMENT AND RESOURCES:

7. **Change Competencies:**
   (For executives, Change Consultants and all employees)

8. **Commitment to the Perseverance Required:**
   (By the CEO, management, Board of Directors and Change Consultant Cadre)

9. **Enterprise-Wide Change Resources:**
   (All types of resources needed are committed to and funded)

EWC YEARLY MAP OF IMPLEMENTATION:

10. **The detailed Map:**
    (Including all Change Leadership Team meetings, the EWC Annual Strategic Review (and Update) and an Enterprise-Wide Change Capacity Review)

EBRSP-8.pmd

1420 Monitor Road • San Diego • California • 92110-1545 • (619) 275-6528 • Fax (619) 275-0324

STEP #9

12 ABSOLUTES FOR SUCCESS IN ENTERPRISE-WIDE CHANGE™

Create A Yearly Strategic Management Cycle –
(Corporate-Wide Core Competency #3)

1. **Have a clear vision and positioning with shared values**—of your Ideal Future in the marketplace.

2. **Develop focused and shared core strategies**—as the *glue* for setting and reviewing annual goal setting and action planning for all major departments/SBUs, with a single page "tri-fold" to communicate the Enterprise-Wide Game Plan.

3. **Set up Quadruple Bottom Line Measures and a Tracking System**—to ensure clarity of purpose and focus on the scoreboard for success. Cascade it down in a Line-of-Sight for accountability of results at all levels – Unit-by-Unit/Dept.-by-Dept.

4. **Focus on the vital few leverage points of Business Excellence based on an Enterprise-Wide assessment of an Organization as a System. Create a Strategic Business Design with Watertight Integrity – Corporate-Wide Core Competency #3.**

5. **Set the Top Enterprise-Wide Change Priorities**—on only 2 pages to focus everyone on what's important next year.

6. **Conduct Large Group Enterprise-Wide Change Review and Critique Meetings**—to ensure that everyone knows and is "in sync" with everyone else.

7. **Institutionalize the Parallel Involvement Process**—with all key stakeholders as the new *participative* way you plan, change, and run your business day-to-day. Create a critical mass for Enterprise-Wide Change—that "goes ballistic" and becomes self-sustaining.

8. **Develop and gain public commitments of "Personal Leadership Plans (PLPs)":** **Develop & Achieve Leadership Excellence – Corporate-Wide Core Competency #1**—by building a Leadership Development System for all supervisory and management leaders to achieve Leadership Excellence.

9. **Redo your HR Management Practices**—to support the positioning and values, especially your high performance management and Rewards system.

continued

12 ABSOLUTES FOR SUCCESS IN ENTERPRISE-WIDE CHANGE™

10. **Establish an Enterprise-Wide Change™ Leadership Team**—led by the CEO and facilitated by a master external facilitator—with a single page, yearly comprehensive map of implementation—that meets on a monthly basis to lead all major changes.

11. **Set up a Program Management Office with "Strategic Sponsorship and/or Change Project Teams"** —of cross-functional leaders to develop, track, and monitor each core strategy. Use innovative Project/Progress Teams as the vehicle for change. Set up an "internal cadre" support team to support the Program Management Office.

12. **Conduct the Annual Enterprise-Wide Review (and Update)**—like an independent financial audit to ensure constant updating of your Enterprise-Wide Game Plan. This process begins to institutionalize **Corporte-Wide Core Competency #2 — "Build an Integrated, Yearly Strategic Management Cycle."**

1420 Monitor Road • San Diego • California • 92110-1545 • (619) 275-6528 • Fax (619) 275-0324

THE CASCADE OF CHANGE
The Systems Thinking Approach™

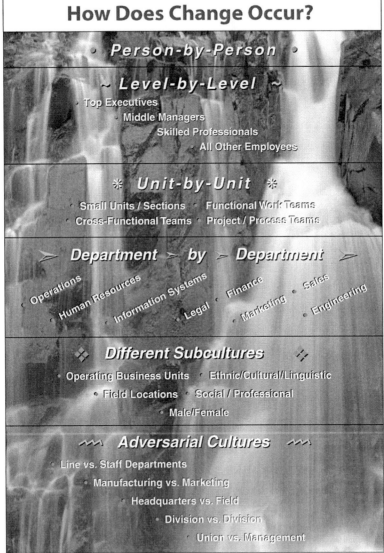

How Does Change Occur?

Person-by-Person

~ Level-by-Level ~
Top Executives
Middle Managers
Skilled Professionals
All Other Employees

Unit-by-Unit
Small Units / Sections • Functional Work Teams
Cross-Functional Teams • Project / Process Teams

Department by Department
Operations
Human Resources
Information Systems
Legal • Finance • Sales
Marketing • Engineering

Different Subcultures
Operating Business Units • Ethnic/Cultural/Linguistic
Field Locations • Social / Professional
Male/Female

Adversarial Cultures
Line vs. Staff Departments
Manufacturing vs. Marketing
Headquarters vs. Field
Division vs. Division
Union vs. Management

MEWC-02

EBRSP-9.pmd

1420 Monitor Road • San Diego • California • 92110-1545 • (619) 275-6528 • Fax (619) 275-0324

ENTERPRISE-WIDE CHANGE™

How to Design, Build, and Sustain Business Excellence and Superior Results

The Systems Thinking Approach™ to Creating Customer Value

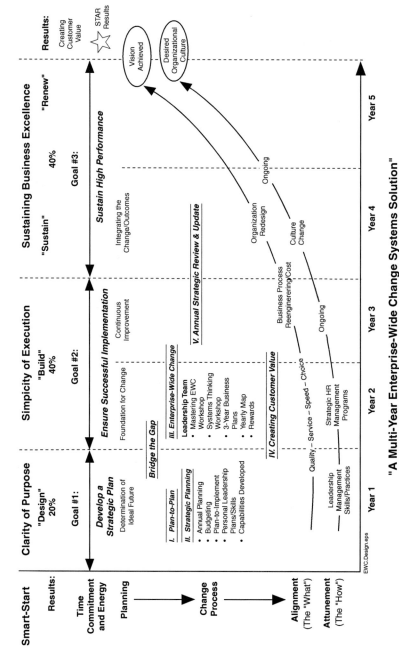

"A Multi-Year Enterprise-Wide Change Systems Solution"

EWC.Design.eps

1420 Monitor Road • San Diego • California • 92110-1545 • (619) 275-6528 • Fax (619) 275-0324

STEP #10

ANNUAL STRATEGIC/EWC REVIEW

Annual Strategic Review

"Similar to a yearly independent financial audit and update"

Goal #1: Assess the Strategic Management Process itself

Goal #2: Assess the status of the Strategic Plan achievement itself

Resulting in Part 2:

1. Updating your Strategic Plan

2. Clarifying your annual planning and strategic budgeting priorities for next year

3. Problem solving any issues raised in either goal

4. Setting in place next year's Annual Plan and Strategic Change Management Process

EBRSP-10.pmd

1420 Monitor Road • San Diego • California • 92110-1545 • (619) 275-6528 • Fax (619) 275-0324

THE ENTERPRISE-WIDE CHANGE™ REVIEW PROCESS

STEPS

1. Contracting and Plan-to-Review

2. Conduct the review and diagnosis

3. Synthesize data, write report, make recommendations

4. Hold a Change Leadership Team two-day meeting to:

   — Receive report and feedback

   — Discuss recommendations

   — Update your Strategic Plan

   — Set priorities for next year's Annual Plans

   — Make decisions for Enterprise-Wide strategic change management Game Plan and actions

   — Make decisions regarding next steps (i.e., Focusing on some Vital Few Leverage Points for Strategic Change)

5. Integrate changes into the (1) monthly Change Leadership Team meetings, (2) specific Enterprise-Wide change projects, as well as (3) day-to-day tasks to achieve our Vision

EBRSP-10.pmd

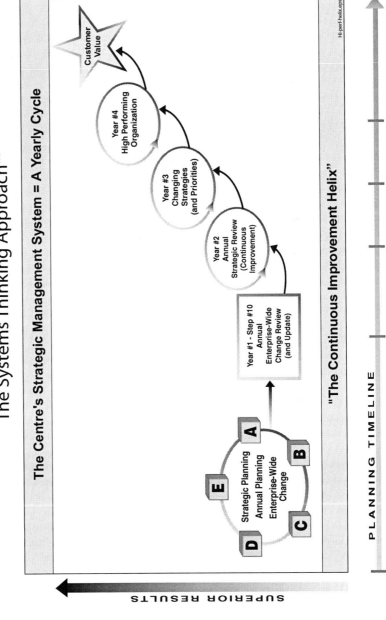

ANNUAL ENTERPRISE-WIDE STRATEGIC REVIEW (AND UPDATE)

HIGH PERFORMING ORGANIZATIONS
The Systems Thinking Approach™

The Centre's Strategic Management System = A Yearly Cycle

Customer Value

Year #4
High Performing Organization

Year #3
Changing Strategies (and Priorities)

Year #2
Annual Strategic Review (Continuous Improvement)

Year #1 - Step #10
Annual Enterprise-Wide Change Review (and Update)

Strategic Planning
Annual Planning
Enterprise-Wide Change

A B C D E

"The Continuous Improvement Helix"

SUPERIOR RESULTS

PLANNING TIMELINE

START   YEAR 1   YEAR 2   YEAR 3   YEAR 4

Hi-perf-helix.eps

EBRSP-10.pmd

1420 Monitor Road • San Diego • California • 92110-1545 • (619) 275-6528 • Fax (619) 275-0324

STRATEGIC MANAGEMENT SYSTEM: IT'S SIMPLE: ENTERPRISE-WIDE CHANGE™

(Once You Use The Systems Thinking Approach™)

The Three Foundational Core Competencies of Every Organization on Earth:

1. Have a Shared Direction

A. Develop a Strategic Plan that is Customer-Focused
- with a shared Vision, Values and Core Strategies, pointing to a clear Future Positioning
- develop focused, organization-wide Action Priorities for the next year

B. Develop Buy-in and Stay-in to the Yearly Strategic Management Cycle and Plan
- communicate – communicate – communicate (stump speeches)
- involvement – participative management – and WIFFM

> **Core Competency #2:** *Build an Integrated Strategic Management System*
> – *"Use Systems Thinking – Focus on the Customer"*

2. Develop and Implement Enterprise-Wide Change

A. Conduct a Strategic Business Assessment and Redesign
- to ensure the fit of all policies and parts, people and business processes of the organization – use *Building on the Baldrige*, a Fast Track Best Practices Assessment
- using the overall direction, Strategic Plan and positioning as the criteria

B. Conduct an Enterprise-Wide Change™ Process to Cascade down department work plans, budgets and accountability with Watertight Integrity and Accountability to the Shared Direction (level/level – unit/unit)
- using the core strategies, action priorities, and values as the glue to make Organization-Wide change down and throughout the organization

> **Core Competency #3:** *Create a Strategic Business Design with Watertight Integrity* –
> *"Systematic problems require system-wide solutions."*

3. Develop Leaders Who Can Successfully Lead and implement Changes in the Shared Direction and Strategic Business Design

A. Know your role(s) as a leader
- **leaders**: focus on content and consequences
- **support cadre**: focus on processes and infra-structure coordination

B. Build follow-up structures and processes
- to track, adjust and achieve the plan and key success measures/results
- to reward, recognize and celebrate progress and results

> **Core Competency #1:** *Develop and Achieve Leadership Excellence* –
> *"Continually increase your range and depth of leadership skills through Leading Strategic Change and Innovation."*

EBRSP-10.pmd

1420 Monitor Road • San Diego • California • 92110-1545 • (619) 275-6528 • Fax (619) 275-0324

BOTTOM LINE

What we think,
or what we know,
or what we believe

is, in the end,
of little consequence.

The only consequence . . .
. . . is what we do!

**Time Management, Team Work, and
Organization Effectiveness**

A systems approach to Strategic Management

(Planning, Leadership, and Change)

is

the **ultimate** time management tool

for

an entire organization.

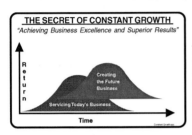

THE SECRET OF CONSTANT GROWTH
"Achieving Business Excellence and Superior Results"

ENHANCE YOUR "STRATEGIC IQ"™!

The Centre's Executive Briefing and Plan-To-Plan is designed to establish a common set of principles and knowledge on the specific Strategic Management project that your organization needs to develop or improve. By using this Systems Thinking Approach™ and principles, you can develop an Enterprise-Wide Game Plan for successful execution. Build your capacity to achieve and sustain business excellence and superior results.

Achieve Organizational Clarity, Simplicity and Superior Results!

EXECUTIVE BRIEFING DAY OUTLINE

AM - Executive Briefing : *"Educating and Assessing"*
- Choose from eight Strategic Managment Topics
- Learn the research on Proven Best Practices
- Assess your organization vs. these Best Practices Management Topics

PM - Plan-To-Plan Tasks: *"Organizing and Tailoring"*
- Organize and engineer success up front
- Tailor the change process to your needs
- Build a practical and realistic "Game Plan"

EIGHT EXECUTIVE BRIEFING DAY TOPICS
Strategic Management: The Systems Thinking Approach™

1. Strategic and Systems Thinking

2. Reinventing Strategic Planning

3. Enterprise-Wide Change

4. Creating the People Edge (Strategic HR Management)

5. Achieving Leadership Excellence

6. Becoming Customer Focused

7. Aligning Delivery & Distribution (Business Planning)

8. Creating Customer Value (Positioning & Design)

Science-Based Proven Research
- We are Interpreters and Translators of Proven Best Practices Research from the *Science of Living Systems*.
- We tailor these Best Practices into powerful, practical and easy to use, simple tools.

THE SYTEMS THINKING APPROACH™
- We own Systems Thinking Press™ the "Premier Publisher and Clearinghouse for Systems Thinking Resources".
- Visit our web site www.SystemsThinkingPress.com
- Learn about ALL our Strategic Management Materials.

NO FURTHER OBLIGATIONS
- There are NO Further Obligations after this day.
- WE will work with you ONLY if we are convinced you are seriously committed to success (why waste time & money)
- Success requires your understanding, discipline, persistence and leadership!

**Systems
Thinking
Press™**

Specialists in Systems Resources
www.SystemsThinkingPress.com

Ordering Information

Send Order Form to: Systems Thinking Press - 1420 Monitor Road - San Diego, CA 92110-1545

Phone: 619-275-6528 - **Fax:** 619-275-0324 - **Email:** info@SystemsThinkingPress.com - **Website:** www.SystemsThinkingPress.com

Date _____   If rush order, need products by _____

Name _____   Title _____

Company _____

Shipping Address _____

City _____   State _____   Postal Code _____   Country _____

Phone _____   Fax _____   Email _____

Quantity	Code	Description	Regular Price	Amount
	EBRSP	Executive Briefing - The ABCs of Strategic Management	call for rates	

Sub Total	
Sales Tax (CA residents only)	
Shipping/handling charges	
TOTAL (payable in US $)	

Payment Method ~ Please Check One

Credit Cards (processed in US Dollars)   Visa   Master Card   America Express   Discover

Credit Card # _____   Expiration Date _____

Name on Card _____   Signature _____

Check or Money Order Enclosed   Purchase Order (only for over $100)   PO# _____

Shipping: Please choose a shipping method below. We make every attempt to ship the cheapest and best method. If you wish to be contacted with the shipping cost prior to your order being shipped, please check here

United States	International		
UPS Ground – 1 ½ weeks/less	Federal Express	International – One week or less	Priority International* – 2-3 days
UPS Three Day (business days)	UPS	International – One week or less	International Expedited* - 2-3 days
UPS Two Day (business days)	US Mail	Global Priority* - 1 ½ weeks or less	Global Express* - One week or less
UPS Next Day (business days)		*Not available in all areas.*	
US Postal Service			

Return Policy

You may return the products within 30 days of receipt for a refund (eProducts are not refundable). Shipping charges will not be refunded. A 20% (or greater) fee may be applied for items returned damaged. To assure proper credit, you must do three things: 1) return materials by a traceable means, 2) include a copy of your invoice, and 3) provide a reason for the return.

Our "Nothing-To-Loose Guarantee"

Our unconditional guarantee of high quality materials: if for any reason you are not satisfied with any of Haines Centre Assessments' materials, you may return them within 30 days for a refund – no questions asked.

We reserve the right to change prices without prior notice.

Systems Thinking Press
1420 Monitor Road · San Diego · CA · 92110-1545 · (619) 275-6528 · Fax (619) 275-0324
www.SystemsThinkingPress.com · Email info@SystemsThinkingPress.com